# The Undefined Lines of 'Ataraxia & Cherish'

## PRANAY SAWARKAR

# The Undefined Lines Of Ataraxia & Cherish

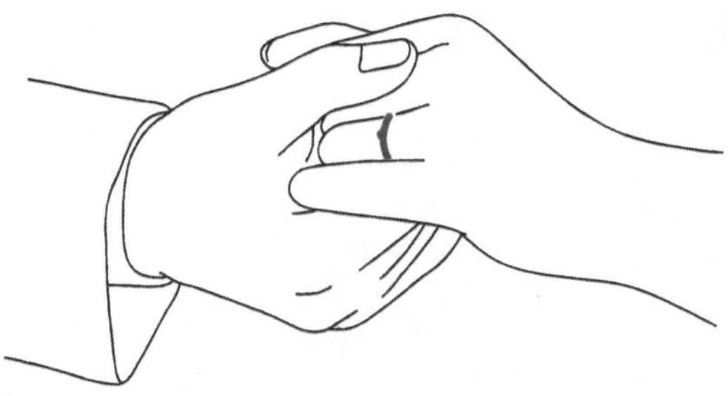

# Pranay Sawarkar

Made with on the Notion Press Platform
www.notionpress.com

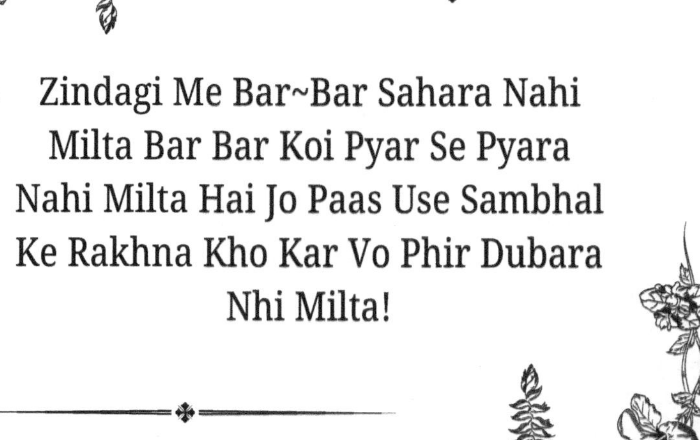

Zindagi Me Bar~Bar Sahara Nahi
Milta Bar Bar Koi Pyar Se Pyara
Nahi Milta Hai Jo Paas Use Sambhal
Ke Rakhna Kho Kar Vo Phir Dubara
Nhi Milta!

# THE CONTENT

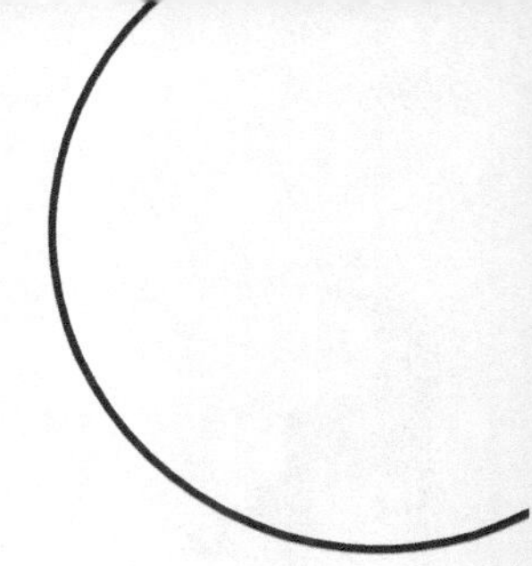

# THE
# CONTENT

# FOREWARD

In a world where love is often simplified, reduced to fleeting moments or hollow declarations, The Undefined Lines of Ataraxia & Cherish dares to explore the raw, unspoken truths that exist beneath the surface. This is not just a story- it's an invitation. An invitation to journey into the heart of two souls: Ataraxia, a being of serene grace, and Cherish, a radiant force whose beauty lies not just in the physical, but in the purity of her essence.

Pranay Sawarkar's words flow like a delicate river, carving paths into unexplored depths, where love is neither black nor white, but a complex shade of untold emotions. Through their union, we witness the alchemy of opposites the calm and the wild, the peace and the passion-intertwining in a symphony that speaks to the heart of human experience. Their love is not bound by rules, but rather, it is shaped by the quiet tension between what is and what could be. It is a love that transcends definition, unafraid of its own ambiguity. It is both chaos and order, a juxtaposition of longing and contentment, where each moment is a delicate balance between surrender and control.

Ataraxia and Cherish are more than characters: they are the personifications of ideals we all strive for: the unattainable peace of mind and the unconditional, perfect beauty of love. Together, they challenge us to ask: What does it mean to truly cherish? How does love evolve when two hearts meet, not in perfect harmony, but in the raw vulnerability of the undefined? Here, love is not a destination but a journey a journey that promises no answers, only experiences, no boundaries, only exploration. In their story, there is a sacredness to the uncertainty, a beauty in the struggle to find meaning in the undefined. This love, both quiet and fierce, speaks the language of the soul.

In these pages, you will be transported into a world where love is both delicate and fierce, where serenity does not come without its storm, and where the flaws of Cherish only make her more radiant. Sawarkar's prose is a mirror- reflecting not only the beauty of the characters but the beauty within each of us, waiting to be discovered, cherished, and understood. It is in their imperfections that we find our own, and in their love, we rediscover the power to heal, to forgive, and to be whole.

This is a story for anyone who has ever dared to love deeply, who has ever yearned for the peace that only a rare connection can bring. It is for the dreamers who know that love is not always clear, but always transformative; for those who understand that the most profound relationships are the ones that are written in the spaces between words. The Undefined Lines of Ataraxia & Cherish will linger long after you turn the last page, leaving you with the quiet, undeniable truth: sometimes, the most beautiful loves are the ones we cannot define.

This book is a celebration of those moments, a testament to love's quiet power to shape the soul and leave an indelible mark on the heart.
As you read, may you be reminded that love, like life itself, is never truly defined—only felt.


PRANAY SAWARKAR
{CO-FOUNDER OF MERHAM}
DATE:- 05/05/2025

# PREFACE

In the tender space between serenity and longing lies a story untold a tale woven not with grand gestures, but with moments that linger quietly in the heart. The Undefined Liens of Ataraxia & Cherish is a journey into such a space a space where love blossoms silently, and beauty is not only seen but deeply felt.

This book is a reflection of the unspoken bonds that form between souls, the undefined connections that defy explanation yet carry the weight of something eternal. At its heart is Cherish a soul so flawless in nature, in thought, in spirit that even the quietest of her gestures ripple across the narrative like poetry in motion. Her beauty is not only external but lives in her grace, her kindness, and the effortless way she exists in the world.

As the story unfolds, so does the delicate thread of love one that grows not with certainty, but with depth, tenderness, and vulnerability. Though incomplete in form, their love is complete in meaning. Through Pranay Sawarkar's evocative prose, readers are invited to feel not just the joy of love, but the ache of its absence, the peace of its presence, and the reverence of remembering someone who once made the world feel still.

Their connection was never loud, never flamboyant. It was in the glances that held time still, in the silences that spoke louder than words, in the way Cherish smiled like sunlight slipping through the cracks of a closed room. She was the chaos in his calm, the softness in his silence. In loving her, he discovered a part of himself that was never truly his until she touched it.

**This is a love letter to all the unfinished stories to the hearts that beat but never belonged, to the souls that met at the wrong time but in the right way. The Undefined Liens of Ataraxia & Cherish is not about happy endings, but about the beauty of having loved, even if only for a while, even if only in fragments. It is about the kind of love that doesn't need to last forever to mean forever.**

# PROLOGUE

Some loves are written in stars, others in scars. Theirs was written in glances fleeting, precious, and powerful enough to echo across lifetimes. There were no grand declarations, no promises carved into stone. And yet, every time they spoke, even in passing. the world around them slowed, like time respected the sacredness of their connection. It wasn't loud love, but it was real the kind that doesn't chase attention, but commands memory.

They would cross paths like verses of an unfinished poem brief, beautiful, and never quite complete. He would watch her from a distance, not because he couldn't reach her, but because some distances are made of respect, not fear. To him, she wasn't someone to possess she was someone to cherish, even from afar. And so he did. Quietly. Devotedly. Every detail about her became sacred. The way she tucked her hair behind her ear. The softness in her eyes when she spoke about the things she loved. The way her presence made even the most ordinary moments feel eternal.

She, perhaps, never knew the depth of what she stirred in him. Maybe she felt it. Maybe she didn't. But love the real kind doesn't always need to be known to be true. Sometimes it's enough that it was felt. Deeply. And in the quietest corners of his heart, he knew that meeting her was not a coincidence. It was a divine interruption. A brief taste of what eternity might feel like. She brought him closer to himself. without ever trying. And that, perhaps, was the most beautiful tragedy of all that the person who made him feel most alive was the one he could never fully have.

Even now, when the world moves on, and time folds itself around new stories, her memory lingers like the scent of rain on dry earth. She became his calm, his chaos, his muse. And in writing these words. he does not seek closure for some stories are not meant to close. They are meant to be remembered. Carried. Lived, again and again, through the echoes they left behind.

This is more than a story. It is a confession. A quiet surrender to the kind of love that redefined what it means to feel. So, if you've ever loved someone in silence, or felt a connection that the world couldn't understand know that you are not alone. This book is for you. For the ache. For the beauty. For the incomplete!!

# THE UNDEFINED LINE OF ATARAXIA & CHERISH

## CHAPTER 1

# When Heart Typed Hello...

# WHEN HEART TYPED HELLO...

### CHAPTER I : HEARTS BEHIND SCREEN

It was the 6th of January, 2021-just another ordinary day in Ataraxia's life. The world was still caught in the quiet chaos of the pandemic. Streets were silent, but hearts were loud on social media. Like many, Ataraxia found himself scrolling through his feed, his mind wandering aimlessly, until a name-no, a face-stopped him cold. Cherish.

It wasn't just a random suggestion. Her face, though now framed in a profile picture, wasn't new to him. He had seen her before-three, maybe four months ago, at a small community event before restrictions tightened again. That evening, she was wearing a simple black dress, her laughter echoing like soft wind chimes, dancing freely under the open sky. Ataraxia remembered how his eyes followed her-not in lust, but in awe. She hadn't noticed him, of course. Why would she? She was the kind of girl who seemed to belong in stories, not real life.

Flawless. Radiant. Almost unreal-like an angel momentarily misplaced on Earth.

He had smiled then, silently, as if saving the moment in his mind like a photograph. There was no conversation, no dramatic incident-just a brush of presence. He remembered once when she had passed by him, the soft breeze carrying her perfume to him-a scent of Lavender and something sweetly mysterious. In that fleeting moment, their eyes met. Just for a second. But something inside him stirred.

**The Thing which I really feel when I saw her First time for few seconds onwards:-.**
*"I used to look at the world through her eyes, it was like there was a burst of color in her mind. For when I would only see the night, she'd show me a city drowning in the light. Her eyes had a spark of the stars and for a brief while I'd forget all my scars!!"*

And now, there she was again. On his screen. Digital, yet just as enchanting.

Hesitantly, he hovered over the "Add Friend" button. His fingers trembled slightly. It felt like too small a gesture for someone so beyond the reach of everyday words. But still, he clicked.

Friend Request Sent.

He tried to forget about it after that, telling himself not to expect a response. People like her-they didn't talk to people like him.

But six hours later, a soft ping broke the silence.

**"Cherish accepted your friend request."**

He stared at the screen in disbelief, heart racing as if fate itself had decided to play a tune for his soul. And then-like magic-came the first message.

Cherish: "Hey, do I know you? You look familiar somehow."

Ataraxia felt his heart smile. He had hoped she'd remember. And now, here was his chance to reply. What started as a few hesitant messages turned into a warm, flowing conversation. They talked about the event -how she remembered losing her way in the parking lot and laughing at her own clumsiness. He recalled helping someone find directions that night; it turned out, unknowingly, he had helped her.

Cherish: "Wait... that was you?, I don't exactly remember you, but yeah, I remember your eyes and will never forget how attractive and charming they are. Seriously, when I saw them, I just felt the attachment with you."

It felt like the beginning of something that neither of them had planned, yet both of them were somehow waiting for.

Their chats grew longer. From memes and music to dreams and fears. The world outside remained locked down, but in those messages, they found a window to something new. Every "hello" felt warmer, every "goodnight" a little harder to say.

Ataraxia found himself waking up looking forward to her words, her laugh in text, her voice notes-soft and sincere. Cherish, too, began to open up. She wasn't just beautiful. She was kind, curious, and layered like poetry waiting to be read slowly.

As days turned into weeks, their connection deepened. Not with fireworks, but with the quiet certainty that something real was unfolding.

Even in the silence between their messages, Ataraxia felt something shift inside him. It wasn't infatuation-not the kind that fades with time-but rather a quiet recognition. Like meeting someone whose story had always been running parallel to yours, just waiting for the pages to finally touch.

They began speaking every day. Sometimes for hours, other times just enough to share a single thought, a song, or a photo of the sky from where they stood. Cherish would often send sunrise pictures from her window, captioned with little thoughts like, "This one looks like it's breathing." Ataraxia, in retum, would send her Quotes he'd never dared to share with anyone else.

One night, well past midnight, she sent him a voice note. Her voice was calm, a little sleepy. but full of something unspoken.

Cherish: "It's strange, isn't it? How you can feel safe with someone you barely know, just because the silence between you doesn't feel heavy?"

Ataraxia listened to that recording twice. Then again. He didn't reply with words-just a single heart emoji, it felt enough. Anything more might've broken the spell.

Days blurred. Time didn't matter anymore. They weren't just talking-they were discovering. Each message a thread, weaving something delicate between two people who had only just dared to believe that maybe, just maybe, they were meant to meet in this strange digital crossing

But as with all beautiful beginnings, there came a pause.

One evening, she didn't reply.

Not immediately. Not for hours. Then a day passed.
**Ataraxia told himself it was nothing People get busy. People need space.**

But the heart doesn't care for logic-it only knows rhythm. And suddenly, that rhythm had been interrupted.

He stared at the last message he had sent: "I found a song that reminded me of you. Want me to send it?"

Seen. No reply

A quiet ache began to bioom in his chest. Not anger. Not fear Just... wonder

Had he imagined it all? The laughter, the connection, the shared vulnerability?

He closed his chat app and turned off his phone

That night, sleep didncome easily

The next morning, the world outside Ataraxia's window seemed greyer than usual. The sky was wrapped in a dull haze, and even the bird song felt distant. He made coffee but didn't drink it. Scrolled aimlessly. Reopened the chat, then closed it again.

But just as he was about to give up on the day entirely, his phone buzzed-three soft vibrations. A voice note.

Cherish

Her voice came through, quiet but steady.

Cherish: "Hey... I'm sorry for the silence. Yesterday was heavy, I didn't know how to say that without sounding like I was pulling away. I wasn't. I'm not. I just needed a day. I guess I forgot how to explain things. when they don't make sense to me either."

A pause. Then a sigh.

Cherish: "But your message? The song? Please still send it. I need music today"

Ataraxia exhaled, a breath he hadn't realized he'd been holding. It wasn't rejection. It wasn't distance. It was life-messy, unpredictable, human.

He quickly replied, attaching the song "I'm glad you're here. Take all the days you need. I'll still be around when you feel like saying 'hi' again.

The song he'd chosen was soft, mostly instrumental, with faint echoes of a woman's voice. humming a lullaby in the background. He didn't explain why it reminded him of her. He knew she'd feel it.

Later that evening, she messaged again.

Cherish: "I listened to it on repeat for an hour. It felt like someone hugging my thoughts."

From then on, something shifted-quietly, beautifully. Their conversations didn't just deepen: they grew gentler. Less like strangers trying to impress each other, more like kindred minds remembering something they once knew. They began exchanging voice notes more than texts. There was warmth in the pauses, intention in the smallest responses.

Cherish told him about her childhood-how she used to write letters to imaginary friends and tuck them in the hollow of a tree in her backyard. Ataraxia confessed he used to name the stars he saw from his roof and believed they whispered back when the wind blew just right.

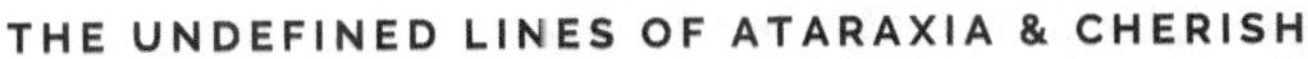

They laughed about these things. Not because they were silly, but because they were sacred-secrets they hadn't shared in years.

And one night, when neither of them could sleep, Ataraxia typed:

"Do you think maybe we were meant to meet when everything else had quieted down?"

Cherish replied instantly

"Maybe the noise had to stop so we could hear each other."

And with that message, the undefined line between two hearts drew just a little clearer.

For the next twenty days, their connection blossomed like a slow, intentional bloom. Morning greetings turned into thoughtful exchanges. Nightly goodbyes carried the weight of everything unsaid. They spoke about books, about places they dreamed of visiting, about fears they rarely admitted to anyone. The kind of honesty that doesn't come often-only when you know the person on the other side won't flinch.

Cherish would sometimes vanish for hours, but always returned with little voice notes like, "Sorry, I was just floating through the day," or "Had to recharge a bit." Ataraxia understood. He never asked for more than she could give.

They even had a little ritual-each night at 11:11, they'd send each other a single wish Sometimes it was silly, like wishing for ice cream with no calories. Other times it was vulnerable, like "I wish I could tell you what I really feel without it coming out messy

But then, on the evening of January 28th, something shifted.

She was online.
Then gone

No message. No emoji. No "be right back."

Ataraxia waited. Told himself not to overthink. Maybe she fell asleep. Maybe she got busy. Maybe her mind needed space again.

But the next day came and went.

And the next

**January 29th.**
Still nothing.

Her chat window showed no activity. No green light. No status updates. Like she had quietly stepped out of the room without closing the door behind her.

Ataraxia kept checking, telling himself it was no big deal. But every hour stretched like a thread pulled too tight. He typed messages he didn't send. "Everything okay?" "Just checking in." "I hope you're safe"

Then deleted them all.

What do you say when someone becomes a part of your days, then disappears without a sound?

He didn't want to be intrusive. But silence, when it comes without warning, is its own kind of noise.

And suddenly, the warmth of their twenty-day bond felt like a memory still sitting warm in his hands-while she had quietly vanished into the unknown

Ataraxia sat by his window that night, watching the moonlight spill over empty streets. The city, once full of noise seemed to mirror his heart-quiet, searching, unfinished. He didn't know where Cherish had gone, or why she'd left without a word. But he wasn't angry.

Some people, he thought, don't disappear to hurt you. They disappear because they're trying to find pieces of themselves they're not ready to show.

Still, in the quiet ache of her absence, he realized something extraordinary.

He missed her not because of how often they spoke, but because of how deeply she had made him feel like someone had finally looked into his world and wanted to stay a while.

And though she was gone, for now, he held on to a single truth

Sometimes, the most beautiful beginnings don't ask for permission. They just happen-like a heartbeat that types "hello," and changes everything without needing a reason.

Ataraxia He doesn't know why he feels like that. Some organ of his body has left his body, and it makes him feel very insecure and go into deep thinking... always thinking about her... It feels like:-

**"The moment when her eyes beg him to sleep, but he is stuck in the silent war between his own mind and heart"**

# THE UNDEFINED LINE OF ATARAXIA & CHERISH

## CHAPTER 2

# Is She Truly Gone?

# WHEN SHE RETURNED ON THE WIND

## CHAPTER II : WHEN SILENCE SPOKE LOUDER THAN DISTANCE

The days of February felt colder than January had ever been-not in temperature, but in touch. Ataraxia's nights, once warmed by digital whispers and Cherish's playful replies, had become long and soundless.
She was gone.

No message. No goodbye. No reason

It was February 8th when the silence finally broke.

Ataraxia was scrolling through his phone, not madly looking for anything, just searching in the spaces where she used to be. And then, like a long-lost note drifting back into a song, there she was

**Cherish "Hey.."**

A single word. So simple, so heavy. So sudden.

His chest sightened. He didn't know whether to be relieved or confused. Their conversation picked up-light, casual like nothing had happened. But something had. She had vanished for days, and he had nearly drowned in the emptiness she left behind

He couldn't stop himself.

**Ataraxia:-"What happened?"**

Her reply came swiftly, wrapped in avoidance.

**Cherish:-"Nothing."**

But he could sense it. Something was unsaid. Something sat in the spaces between her sentences. Something she wanted to tell-but couldn't.

(In truth, Cherish had wrestled with herself. She wanted to explain, to let him in. But fear is a stubborn gatekeeper, and her heart was not ready to be read.)

She tried to smile through text.

Cherish:-"You must've forgotten me by now, right?"

His fingers paused on the screen.

Ataraxia:-"No... why would !?"

Her words trembled even through pixels.

Cherish:-"We're just friends. So, I thought..."

Just friends.

The phrase echoed. Heavy. Light. Confusing.

But he didn't argue. Not yet. Instead, he returned her soft attempt at normalcy with gentle understanding. Their chat resumed with small talk-clumsy, careful, and quietly meaningful.

Valentine's Day arrived like an uninvited truth.

Ataraxia stared at his screen for a long time before typing: **"Happy Valentine's Day, Cherish."**

It wasn't flirtation. It wasn't declaration. Just a message-a piece of warmth offered without expectation.

Her reply didn't come the way he thought it would.

Cherish:-"My sister knows you."

He blinked. That was unexpected.

She explained vaguely that her sister had seen their chats, or heard about him somehow. And now, that sister had formed an opinion: Ataraxia was someone Cherish shouldn't talk to.

He felt the sting. Not because of the accusation, but because of the distance it threatened to create.

Still, he replied calmly:

Ataraxia: "We're just friends."

But inside, he wished she had defended him before he had to.

He wished she had told her sister how he waited for her during the silence. How he crafted unsent messages like prayers. How he missed her-not just her replies, but her presence.

He didn't say all that..

He just kept talking.

And thankfully, so did she.

Cherish's sister wasn't done. Days later, she inserted herself again-this time more directly. Her tone was sharp, suspicious. Ataraxia didn't fight. He explained. Gently. Honestly.

THE UNDEFINED LINES OF ATARAXIA & CHERISH

But she didn't listen.

Worse, she took the story to Ataraxia's sister. And now the tangled thread stretched between two families.

So Ataraxia sat down with his sister and unfolded the truth like a letter: Every message. Every emotion. Every silence.

His sister listened. Understood. Stood by him.

The storm settled-but something was still tender beneath the surface.

Then came the message that changed everything.

**"I want to tell you something... Can we talk? On a call?"**

Ataraxia's fingers hesitated before typing: "Yes. What time?"

**"7:30 PM."**

That evening, time slowed. His heartbeat was loud. At 7:30 sharp, the call came.

He answered.

And then... he heard her voice.

Sweet. Gentle. A melody wrapped in hesitation.

It wasn't just a sound-it was a feeling. It was the echo of everything her texts had never been able to carry. She laughed nervously, stumbled over her thoughts, paused often-but he was lost in the rhythm of her.

**Cherish shared small things-things that mattered to her, the tender corners of her world. She told him how she loved to draw, often sketching late into the night when the world felt too loud and her thoughts needed a canvas. She sent him photos-some unfinished, some bursting with color. They weren't just images. They were pieces of her-raw, emotional, beautiful.**

*She told him she wrote poems too. Not for anyone else, just for herself. Her words were quiet, like the wind through leaves. Sometimes, she'd send a few lines to Ataraxia, and he'd read them over and over, trying to catch the rhythm of her heart hidden between the stanzas.*

And she sang.

**God, how she sang.**

Sometimes during a voice note, she'd hum a few lines from a song-her voice carrying something fragile, something sincere. It wasn't perfect, but that was what made it real. And addictive. There was always this aching honesty in how she sang-like she wasn't just singing words, but bleeding truths.

One day, she said, almost shyly, "I've told you more about me than I've told most of my friends."

Ataraxia didn't answer right away. But in his silence was something stronger than words: understanding.

She started introducing him to her circle of online friends-people she'd known for a while. Not many. Just a few. Carefully chosen.

Ataraxia talked to them occasionally-sometimes in group chats, sometimes one-on-one. Slowly, he became part of that little digital circle. It was strange at first. Like stepping into someone else's diary. But he held it gently, never pushing, never trying too hard.

Through them, he saw a different version of Cherish-playful, sarcastic, sometimes withdrawn, sometimes wild. He liked every version. Because each one was her.

They laughed over silly things. Shared songs. Memes. Late-night rants. She told him about her brother too -how he was the quiet protector type, always watching but rarely speaking.

Every thread of her life she allowed him to touch felt like a blessing.

And Ataraxia? He was still careful. Still holding back pieces of his heart, unsure if it was right to fall. But he also knew this wasn't just digital friendship anymore. Not to him.

There was something sacred in their connection. And even if they never named it, it was there. Breathing. Waiting

Maybe she didn't feel it the same way.

Or maybe she did.

And just wasn't ready to say it.

The days went by quietly, yet each carried its own meaning.

There were no declarations. No grand gestures. But something about their rhythm-how they showed up in each other's lives, how they listened, how they remembered-felt more intimate than most love stories.

One night, around 1:00 am, after a long talk with their mutual friends, Cherish messaged him privately.

Cherish:
**"Do you ever feel like some people aren't meant to be explained to the world? Like they're only meant to be understood by you?"**

Ataraxia stared at the screen, the glow of the message casting a soft light on his tired face. It took him a moment to reply.

Ataraxia:
**"Maybe. Or maybe the world doesn't deserve to understand them the way we do."**

He could almost feel her smile in the pause that followed. She didn't reply in words, just sent a voice note-only three seconds.

A breath. A soft exhale. Maybe a half-laugh.

She wasn't always consistent. There were days she disappeared again-not like before, not entirely-but she'd go quiet for hours, sometimes a whole day. And he tried not to let his thoughts spiral. He reminded himself: She's like that. She needs space. Let her have it.

**And she always came back.**
**With a story. A drawing. A line of poetry. A song she couldn't get out of her head. And always, that same soft presence that pulled him in like the tide.**

He didn't ask for more. Not because he didn't want more but because he feared asking would break whatever delicate thread they were walking on.

But inside him, something had changed. He wasn't just getting attached to a person.

He was falling for a presence.

The way she filled the silence. The way she understood things without needing context. The way her words stayed with him long after the conversation ended.

And yet, he still didn't say it.

Not aloud.

Not yet.

Because sometimes, the most real feelings grow quietly without announcement, without approval. Just two hearts learning each other's language.

Time passed, and something inside Ataraxia grew heavier. He knew he couldn't keep walking that thin line between almost and never. Not when every poem she shared with him felt like a whisper meant for his soul. Not when her silences started hurting more than her words could ever soothe.

So, he did what writers do best-he wrote.

It wasn't a message. Not a confession. Not even a conversation.

*It was a story, posted quietly to his feed. It looked like fiction to everyone else. But between the metaphors, under the poetry, hidden in the folds of the language-was the truth.*

A truth only one person could see.

**The story spoke of a boy who watched the stars every night, not to count them, but to find the one that blinked in her rhythm. A boy who never confessed in loud declarations, but in carefully chosen silences. And a girl who didn't know how deeply her light had become his sky.**

He ended the story with a line that trembled in honesty..

**"Some people write poems. Others become them."**

He knew she'd read it.

And she did.

Later that night, she messaged him.

**"Was that... about me?"**

He waited a beat, then replied:

**"Only the parts that mattered."**

There was a pause. Not long. Just enough to change the temperature of the night.

Then she answered:

**"I'm sorry, but... I can't. We're just friends. That's all we can be."**

He didn't fight it.

He didn't beg.

But somewhere inside him, something gently collapsed.

It didn't end there.

As if fate wasn't done unraveling the thread, her sister found out. Again.

And this time, she wasn't quiet. She came to him-angry, fierce, unrelenting.

"You need to stop. This is not going anywhere. You're confusing her, and it's unfair."

Ataraxia tried to explain, calmly, honestly.

**"I never forced anything. I just wrote what I felt. That's all."**

But she wouldn't listen.

She told Cherish to cut all contact. To block him. To deactivate everything.

And this time... Cherish listened.

No goodbye.

No explanation

Just silence

On that time, Ataraxia feels that he do something wrong because of that one story; everything has been destroyed, and he feels that there is no more now.....

**<u>So he realized at that moment:</u>**
**"Khuda Kabhi Kisi Pe,**
**Fida Na Karey,**
**Agar Karey Toh,**
**Qayamat Tak Juda Na Karey!!"**

One morning, Ataraxia woke up to find her gone.

Messages unsent. Profile vanished. Like she never existed.

A ghost in the algorithm.

The echo of a voice that once brought warmth now replaced with a void colder than he imagined.

He sat in the clark that night, the weight of her absence pressing against his ribs like a locked door.

Maybe he had been foolish to write that story.

Maybe honesty wasn't always beautiful.

Maybe timing had betrayed him again.

But even in the pain, he didn't regret it.

Because for a moment, he had touched something real

Even if it slipped through his fingers like stardust.

And so, with the screen glowing in the silence, Ataraxia opened a blank note and began to type:

**"She left without a goodbye.
But I'm still here... writing her name into every line I'll never send."**

He hit save

Not to remember her.

But to wait.

Because deep down, a voice whispered-
It was late one night when Ataraxia stared at their chat and whispered to himself, barely audible:

"You're not just a chapter, Cherish.
You're the ink that makes me write!!."

He didn't send it.
But maybe... she already knew.

**THE UNDEFINED LINES OF ATARAXIA & CHERISH**

# THE STRANGER WHO KNEW MY HEART

### CHAPTER III : A VOICE HE ALREADY KNEW

After Cherish vanished, days passed like seasons without sun. Ataraxia waited—at first with hope, then with hurt. Every evening, he'd open the app just to see if she was online. She never was. He messaged once. Twice. Then stopped.

He even tried to reach out to some of her friends. But the silence was louder than ever.

No replies. No sign. No way in.

*"Some goodbyes are never spoken. They are simply felt in silence."*

And so, Ataraxia carried her absence like an invisible wound. He didn't talk about it. But it showed—in his lack of sleep, in his distracted thoughts, in the way he stared longer at the void of his screen.

**The silence wasn't loud anymore. It was heavy. Like a weight pressing on his thoughts, flattening every hope with the same question: *Where did she go?***

Then one day, a friend request appeared.

It was from an account that looked vaguely familiar. The name didn't ring any bells, but something about it stirred a strange feeling—like déjà vu wrapped in mystery.

He ignored it for two or three days, thinking maybe it was a spam account or someone random. But something made him accept it.

**Request accepted.**

And then, a message:
**"Hey. Do I know you from somewhere?"**

Innocent. Vague. But it pulled something in him.

He replied politely, as one would to a complete stranger.

**"Hmm... Not sure. Your name seems familiar though."**

The conversation started slowly. Awkward, even. Just like any new chat.

But something was *off*. Or maybe *too on point*.

The way she messaged the pace, the pauses, the emojis it tugged at his memory. Like a perfume you can't quite place but makes your heart skip.

They talked again the next day.

And the next.

 Until, one afternoon, she asked him:
**"Are you single?"**

Ataraxia raised an eyebrow at his screen, half-smirking.

**"Why? Planning to matchmake me with someone?"**

She replied with an emoji and another question:
**"So tell me... who was your first crush?"**

He laughed. It felt absurdly familiar—the way she teased, the way she typed, the things she asked.

**THE UNDEFINED LINES OF ATARAXIA & CHERISH**

He played along, dodging the questions with dramatic mystery.

"That's classified. You'll need security clearance."

"Or maybe just charm?" she sent back.

The back-and-forth had a rhythm now. A playful banter laced with something deeper. Something hidden.

Then one evening, after a particularly flirtatious exchange, he paused and thought:

*No way... this can't be.*

But his heart whispered: What if it is?

So he asked, casually cloaked in jest:

**"You remind me of someone I used to know. Are you sure we haven't met before?"**

She dodged.

**"Maybe in another lifetime."**

Another joke. Another emoji. Another clue.

But Ataraxia's heart wasn't laughing

He started noticing the small things: her use of certain phrases, the way she sometimes paused for a full day before replying to a joke, only to return with a perfectly timed punchline.

It was her. It *had* to be.

He couldn't prove it. Not yet.
But 95% of him believed it.

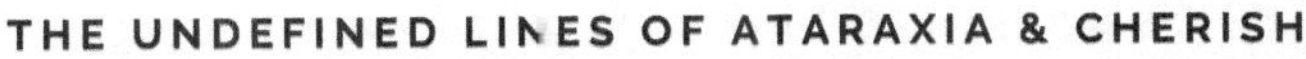

So he tested her-slipping in old references, inside jokes only Cherish would recognize.

She didn't take the bait.

But she didn't flinch either.

Then one night, in a moment too quiet to ignore, he typed:
**"Tell me honestly. Are you... Cherish?"**

Her reply took ten full minutes.

When it came, it was just:
**"Why do you think that?"**

He leaned back in his chair, half-laughing, half-sinking into disbelief.

"Because no one else could annoy me and comfort me at the same time like this."

**"Why are you asking all this?"**

**"No reason. Just curious."**

She kept playing the role of a stranger, but her questions told another story.

And Ataraxia played along-half smiling, half aching.

***"Sometimes we pretend not to know someone because pretending hurts less than knowing they're gone."***

They continued talking like that for weeks.

Every conversation was a careful dance her pretending, him pretending not to know she was pretending.

And then, after almost 30 days, it happened.

Then, like a twist in a movie that had been playing on loop, Cherish came back.

Not as the stranger.
But as herself.

Her original account popped up again. She had reactivated it.

Ataraxia saw the notification and froze. His heart skipped.

**He sent her a request again.**

But she didn't accept it. Not for three days,

And when she finally did, their conversation began not with "Hi" or "I missed you" but with confusion, humor, and just a dash of passive-aggressive sarcasm.

Ataraxia asked the question that was burning in his chest.

**"That other ID... that was yours, right?"**

**"I don't know who she was,"** Cherish replied. **"You seem to have many friends."**

He blinked at the screen. She was dodging again. Or maybe teasing.

**"Why didn't you talk to me earlier?"** *he asked gently.*

She hesitated.

**"I thought... if I stopped talking to you, maybe you'd move on. Make new friends. You're good at that. Right?"**

He didn't answer.

*Because what could he say? That he didn't move on? That every new chat felt like a hollow substitute? That no one typed the way she did? That no one understood his silences the way she did?*

She didn't want an explanation. She just wanted to say:
**"You're bad."**

It made him laugh.

He tried, again, to explain how he felt. Not with pressure. Not with drama. Just honesty.

But once again, she gently turned him down.
**"We're friends, Ataraxia. That's all we can be."**

And yet, she kept talking to him.

Told him stories about boys flooding her DMs. Laughed about how annoying it was. Even teased Ataraxia about being jealous.

(And he was. A little. Okay—a lot.)

*"Jealousy isn't always about possession. Sometimes it's about the fear of being forgotten."*

Still, he smiled through it.

*Because being in her world, even as "just a friend," was better than being nowhere at all.*

The summer drifted by lazy days filled with stolen conversations, late-night jokes, and quiet longing.

Then came school reopening.
Schedules changed.

Cherish got admitted to a different school. She told him casually like it didn't sting.

**"We're not in the same class anymore,"** she said.
**"I am one class ahead of you, you know it right?."**

That made it worse somehow. Close... but unreachable.

Then, she made an announcement.

**"I'm quitting social media. School's hectic. No more online distractions."**

Before Ataraxia could say anything, she added:
**"But here's my number."**

His heart fluttered.

But it didn't last long

**"Also," she said, "since school's started, we shouldn't talk too much. Just focus on studies, okay?"**

He swallowed the ache rising in his throat.

And once again, he asked, carefully:
**"Cherish... can you tell me what this is? Are we just friends? Or something else?"**

She paused.

**"You're asking again?"**

He nodded, even though she couldn't see.

**"I need to know."**

But the answer was the same.

**"I'm sorry... but it's just friendship."**

He accepted it.
Sort of.
Time passed.

They talked. Less, but still meaningful.
Then, one night, the unexpected happened.

She texted him-long, unprompted.

**"Do you remember the story you once wrote? The one where a boy fell for a star that didn't know how to shine for just one person?"**

*He remembered.*
*He remembered everything.*

"I wrote a reply," she said. "I wanted to send it back then but I was scared"

Her poetry:

---

***Tumse baat karna pasand hai, par karte nahi.***
*Lagta hai dil ko ke tumse ho jaayegi mohabbat...*
*Jataate nahi, par lagta hai ke lag gayi hai dil ko tumhaari aadat...*

***Tum aadat ban gaye ho meri, mushkil hai tumse doori banana.***
*Tum saath raho hamesha, aisa lagta hai*
*Par sochte hain, kya kahega zamaana...*

***Tum chahat ban sakte ho meri, mohabbat nahi, par tumpe hai poora bharosa...***
*Hum dost hi theek hain*
*Chahti hoon ke dost hi rahein, hamesha!!*

---

(It spoke of a boy who wrote stories not to impress, but to remember. A boy who used silence like punctuation. A boy whose heart had been quietly waiting behind every word.)

**Ataraxia read the poem over and over.**

*She remembered.*
*She had always remembered.*

**But did that mean something?**
**He didn't know.**

All he knew was that this wasn't the end.

Just a comma.

No reply.
No follow-up.

Just silence.

*"Sometimes, the hardest part isn't the goodbye. It's the moment just before... when everything is still unsaid."*

And with that, the chapter closed,
But not the story.

Because Ataraxia knew—when poetry returns, so does the poet.

**And somewhere in that poem was a key...**
**To a door yet unopened.**

# THE PAUSE BETWEEN HEARTBEATS

### CHAPTER IV : A GOODBYE WITH A DEADLINE

**"*Some goodbyes are not really farewells, but soft silences waiting to be undone.*"**

Six days. That's how long silence had wrapped its fingers around us-soft at first, like a whisper, but tightening slowly like a noose. It wasn't the kind of silence that brings peace. It was the kind that unsettles you, that fills the spaces between thoughts with echoes you can't ignore.

The calendar flipped like it always does, indifferent to the emotional gravity of dates. And just like that, it was **May 23rd—Cherish's birthday.**

Ataraxia had waited for this day with a heart full of unspoken things. He had written a message so long it could've passed for a letter in another era. Each word was picked carefully, almost poetically. But that wasn't enough. He didn't want to just send something. He wanted her to hear it.

From the moment the clock struck 12, he stared at his phone. Should he call? Should he not? He went back and forth with himself like a pendulum fighting gravity. At 1:00 AM, he finally dialed her number-heart racing, breath unsteady.

She answered.
A sleepy but soft "Hello?"
"Happy Birthday, Cherish..." he said.

Just a few soft-spoken words between them—fleeting and tender.
Then, came the real gift.
A message crafted from the pieces of his soul—each word a candle in the dark.

**Massage Send :**

*—A Whisper from the Heart—*

*Today, the sun rose with a little more grace,*
*As if it knew it had to shine upon your face.*
*The breeze hummed softer, the sky blushed blue,*
*Because this world became brighter the moment it got you.*

*A thousand candles couldn't match your light,*
*You turn ordinary days into something bright.*
*You laugh—and the stars pause mid-flight,*
*You smile—and even sorrow turns polite.*

*It's your day, a page of golden hue,*
*So let me take this moment to celebrate you.*
*Not just for the years you've grown through,*
*But for the way you make everything feel new.*

*You're not just beautiful—though that much is true,*
*You're the kind of soul that kindness clings to.*
*You walk into rooms like morning through glass,*
*Softly, surely—making every moment last.*

*You are poetry written in human form,*
*A gentle heart wrapped in the calm of a storm.*
*A dreamer's dream and a lover's grace,*
*The kind of magic time can't erase.*

*On this birthday, I hope you see,*
*How cherished you are, not just by me.*
*But by life itself, which chose to unfold,*
*Another chapter of you, more precious than gold.*

*May joy wrap around you like your favorite song,*
*May every right replace every wrong.*
*May your laughter echo through the years,*
*And your heart forget all silent tears.*

*Today, I wish for skies without grey,*
*For hands that hold and never stray.*
*For midnight talks and morning light,*
*For a soul that sleeps in love each night.*

*I hope you dance with no fear in your step,*
*And gather dreams that others once left.*
*I hope you bloom like spring in full art,*
*With petals unfolding from your heart.*

*You deserve the sun and the rain,*
*The gentle warmth and even the pain—*
*Because from every storm you've walked through,*
*A rainbow now walks inside you.*

*Your heart—oh, it's a sacred place,*
*Where even broken things find grace.*
*You make silence feel like a song,*
*You make the timid feel strong.*

*This day, let the world pause and see,*
*What you've always meant to me.*
*Not just a favorite girl by name,*
*But a soul who set my stars aflame.*

*So, here's to you—to your laugh, your tears,*
*To your story written through the years.*
*To the late-night thoughts and morning sun,*
*To battles lost and wars you won.*

*To the dreams you chase with steady breath,*
*To the love you give without regret.*

*To the way your kindness never fades,*
*Even when the light itself betrays.*

*On your birthday, let life repay,*
*The love you've given without delay.*
*Let every candle on your cake declare:*
*The world is better because you're there.*

*You're not just someone I admire from afar,*
*You're the wish I whisper to every star.*
*You're the reason behind many of my sighs,*
*And the calm behind my wildest skies.*

*Today is yours—take it in full stride,*
*Hold your head high, let your soul glide.*
*Know that somewhere, someone's heart sings,*
*Because your name gives his silence wings.*

*So here's to another year around the sun,*
*May it be your best, your brightest one.*
*And if ever the world feels heavy, unsure—*
*Remember, you're rare... and that's your cure.*

*You're my favorite rhythm, my unwritten line,*
*The pulse in a poem that never stops time.*
*So Happy Birthday, to you, my muse, my light—*
*May your life always be wrapped in delight.*

The next morning, she replied with warmth and happiness. Her message wasn't long, but full of joy.
She was genuinely touched.

*"Some birthdays are remembered not for the gifts, but for the courage it takes to dial a number at 1:00 AM."*

And for a moment, time rewound.

**THE UNDEFINED LINES OF ATARAXIA & CHERISH**

But like every season, May faded.
They talked less. Some days offered 30 minutes of warmth; some none at all.

Two months passed like a blur of quiet.
Cherish focused on her studies. Ataraxia tried, too.
But some memories don't respect silence.

**"Even when I forget the date, my heart remembers you."**

In those rare moments, they'd joke. Or drift into emotional confessions.
And once, briefly, another girl entered their story—
A fleeting accident, not worth a paragraph more.
Because this story belongs to Cherish.
And to Ataraxia, she always will.

Life moved gently. Until one day—

A message from her.
Short. Direct. Like a quiet arrow to the heart.

"Ataraxia... we need to pause. My board exams are near. Can we talk again after eight months?"

He froze.
Eight months?
Even oceans didn't feel this wide.

He pleaded, gently.
"We only talk for 30 minutes... that too, not every day.
We're just friends, right?
 Then why this?"

But sometimes, even love cannot bend will.

Arguments followed.
Not loud. But sharp.
And Ataraxia realized—her decision was already made.

Then he said softly,
"Can I ask for just one thing?"

"What?"

"Can we meet... once?"

They had chosen dates before. All cancelled like broken promises.
But this time, they fixed one—
**September 5.**

The day circled in his heart like a vow.

For the first time... he would see Cherish, not through a screen, not in a dream,
but in real life.
Would it begin anew... or finally end?

He didn't know.
But he knew this:

***"Some people you meet once. Some people you never forget. But some—some live
between the two."***

As she signed off, silence wrapped the night again.

Until finally...
September 5.

A date circled in red ink in the diary of two hearts.

The day they'd finally meet.
The first time Ataraxia would see Cherish—not through a screen,
Not through texts—but in person.

No filters.
No typing indicators.
Just eyes. Voice. Distance... finally closed.

**THE UNDEFINED LINES OF ATARAXIA & CHERISH**

Now, as that September approaches,
Ataraxia wonders:
Will this meeting change everything?
Or will it mark the end of a delicate thread they both held on to?

Will the feelings still be real in the same air?
Will Cherish feel the same?
Will their undefined bond finally find a name...
Or fade into a beautiful memory?

**"Some hearts are meant to meet in silence,**
**And some promises—are tested when finally heard in person."**

As the sun rises on the day they planned,
One question lingers louder than the rest:

**Will this September fulfill the promise they once made,**
**Or will it be the month they quietly part forever?**

**THE UNDEFINED LINES OF ATARAXIA & CHERISH**

# WHEN I SAW HER FIRST TIME..

## CHAPTER V : THE DAY DISTANCE DISAPPEARED

{A tale where one glance lasted an eternity, and a single meeting redefined everything.}

The morning of **5th September** rose with a strange stillness in the heart of Ataraxia. It wasn't just another date marked on a calendar. No—it was a silent symphony of nerves, memories, and unspoken hopes.

He had rehearsed it a hundred times in his mind. The words. The smile. The way he'd greet her. But when the hour arrived, everything fell away. As planned, they had called briefly to confirm the place. A cozy café, quiet and tucked into a corner of the city, like a secret waiting to be found.

Ataraxia reached first. Every tick of the clock tapped against his ribcage. He sat at a table beside the window, trying to calm the sea inside him. And then... she arrived.

**Cherish.**

The café door opened, and for a moment—just one fleeting, breathtaking moment—time held its breath.

She walked in, her presence softer than the breeze yet louder than thunder in his heart.

Her hair fell like cascading poetry, each strand telling stories of days he'd longed for her voice. Her eyes, shimmering with a quiet depth, scanned the room until they found his. And then... she smiled.

That smile. It wasn't just an expression—it was a moment of magic written on her lips.
*"Some people walk in and light up a room. Others walk in, and everything else forgets how to shine."*

Ataraxia stood up, a little awkwardly, caught between disbelief and admiration. She walked toward him with a gentle confidence, her footsteps somehow louder than the café's hum.

She reached the table, softly tapped her finger on his hand, and said,
**"Heyy..."**
That single word, delivered with her signature lilt, melted every shard of hesitation he held.

He offered her a flower bouquet—nothing grand, but full of meaning. She accepted it with a delicate smile that made his pulse skip. He pulled back her chair for her, trying to steady his strembling hands. And then... silence.

They sat across from each other, not speaking. For 5–10 minutes, their eyes did all the talking. It was not an awkward silence—it was sacred. Like the universe had paused to let them breathe each other in.

Ataraxia felt goosebumps race down his spine. Every time her eyes met his, he had to look away—overwhelmed, awestruck, lost.

Then, the waiter arrived to break the enchantment. Ataraxia handed the menu to Cherish and said,
**"You choose."**
She browsed, ordered something simple, and the moment shifted gently into conversation.

They started slow—school, friends, the old days. But then she said something that left a mark:

**"Yes, we're just friends... but it's hard. Really hard. To stay away from someone you once shared so much with. But success is important too. That's why I needed space."**

Ataraxia nodded, understanding the logic but wounded by the heart's rebellion.
They spoke a little more—teasingly, tenderly, carefully.

Cherish looked at him gently and asked with a soft smile,
**"So... how am I looking?"**

Ataraxia was quiet—
Not because he didn't want to answer,
But because there were no words in the universe
That could do justice to how beautiful she looked in that moment.

She laughed lightly and nudged him.
**"You write the best quotes and poetry,"** she said,
**"So shouldn't something be written for me too—right now? Or maybe, whenever you feel like it."**

Ataraxia hesitated.
There was nothing he could say—
Not because he hadn't prepared anything,
But because everything he had prepared had suddenly slipped away.
He had practiced the words at home,
Thought of what he'd say when this moment came,
But now, facing her glow,
His mind was simply... blank.

**"I'm sorry,"** he whispered, a bit flustered.
**"Nothing I say right now can define you."**

Cherish tilted her head playfully and replied,
**"Am I really this much bad?"**

He shook his head instantly.
**"No, no—not at all. Wait a second.**

Then, with trembling hands and a quiet breath,
Ataraxia opened his notes—
He looked into her eyes,
**<u>And softly read :</u>**

*"Tareef kya karu is chaand ki,*

*Tu Khoobsurat chaand se bhi zyada hai.*

*Mehek gulab ki kuch bhi nahi,*

*Tere aage Har baag sada hai.*

*Aur Nasha kuch aisa chda teri nigahon ka mujh par,*

*Ki Ab zindagi bhar hosh mein na aane ka iraada hai.!!"*

As his voice faded into the quiet air,
the last line of his poetry lingering like a soft echo between them,
Cherish didn't speak right away.

She looked at him—
not just with her eyes,
but with that unspoken gaze only someone truly seen can give.
Her lips parted, ever so slightly,
as if words wanted to escape... but couldn't match the warmth rising within her.

Then came that smile—
the one that curved slowly,
like the first light of dawn kissing the earth.
Her cheeks turned a shade of rose the sky would envy,
and she looked down for a second,
trying to hide the blush that had bloomed too fast.

Her fingers reached up, brushing a strand of hair behind her ear—
a gentle nervous gesture.
She bit her lower lip,
not from shyness,
but from the overwhelming feeling
of being known...

THE UNDEFINED LINES OF ATARAXIA & CHERISH

of being adored...
and of being seen in a way she had always wished for.

**"You really wrote that for me?"** she asked softly, her voice nearly a whisper,
as if afraid that speaking louder might break the magic in the air.

Ataraxia nodded, gently,
watching her as though she were a verse still being written.

She stepped a little closer,
not needing to say more.
In that moment, her eyes said it all—
gratitude, wonder, a quiet kind of love.

And even the wind, for a moment,
seemed to pause in reverence.

As the clock approached **2:43 PM**, Cherish glanced at her phone.
**"I have to go. There's some work waiting."**
Ataraxia stood as she prepared to leave. And just before she turned...

**"Take care"**, he said, voice low but steady.
**"Don't worry... I'm always with you."**

But as she walked away, what lingered was not just her silhouette—it was the
imprint she left on every corner of his soul. That first real glimpse of Cherish
was more than enough to ignite a thousand unwritten pages.

So now, let us pause and see her—not through Ataraxia's trembling voice, but
through his unwavering heart.

## A Portrait of Cherish:

Her **eyes**—deep, like a forgotten lake in a forest where only stars whisper.
Mysterious and knowing, they didn't just look; they listened.

Her **smile**—it wasn't wide or exaggerated. It was warm, subtle, like a candle in a room full of Cold. It said things she never dared to say aloud.

Her **voice**—softer than dusk, with an odd power to calm storms or raise tides depending on the words she chose.

Her **hair**—a cascade of midnight poetry, sometimes shy, sometimes wild, always beautiful.

Her **tone**—a mix of innocence and hidden mischief, like she always knew something you didn't.

Her **gestures**—small, gentle, unintentional things. Tucking her hair behind her ear. Tilting her head when curious. Smiling without meaning to

In more word to say that :

Ataraxia sat quietly, her eyes never leaving Cherish. There was something magical about her-
Cherish wasn't just a girl, she was a vision, a living work of art. Every little detail about her seemed perfect in its own way

Cherish's lips were the first thing Ataraxia noticed. They were soft and gently curved, like the petals of a rose. They weren't too full, yet they held a beauty that made them seem almost perfect. Her lips were a soft pink, a natural color, like the first blush of dawn. When she smiled, Ataraxia could almost hear a story being told, one that only her heart could understand. It was a smile that felt like a secret waiting to be discovered.

Her cheeks added to the charm, with a soft glow that reminded Ataraxia of the warmth of a summer day. There was a natural flush to them, a soft pink that made Cherish look like she had been kissed by the sun. Her cheeks weren't too sharp, just enough to give her face a gentle, rounded shape. When she smiled, her cheeks seemed to lift even more, giving her face a youthful yet graceful look that was impossible to ignore.

But it was her eyes that truly captured Ataraxia's heart. They were deep, rich brown, like dark pools of melted chocolate There was something magical about them-flickers of gold in her eyes. that made them sparkle with every movement Cherish's eyes were full of emotions, speaking volumes without a single word When she looked at something with love or care, her eyes softened in a way that made you feel as though you could look into her soul. The way her lashes fluttered, so delicate, added a softness to her gaze that seemed endless.

Cherish's hair was another part of her beauty that Ataraxia couldn't stop staring at. It was dark. and smooth, falling in soft waves that framed her face like a curtain of silk. It shone, catching the light in a way that made it almost look alive, as though it had a beauty of its own. Every time Cherish moved, her hair would shift and sway, creating a soft, graceful flow that only added to her charm. Ataraxia could barely take her eyes off it.

Her skin was flawless, glowing with a soft, warm radiance. It looked smooth, like porcelain, with a golden hint that made it seem as though Cherish was always bathed in sunlight. Her skin was perfect to the touch, soft and warm, like the feeling of a gentle breeze on your skin. Ataraxia couldn't help but be drawn to it, to the way her skin seemed to hold the light, making her look as though she had been kissed by the earth itself.

Cherish wasn't just a beautiful girl  she was the embodiment of grace, warmth, and elegance. Every part of her, from her lips to her skin, was a quiet promise of beauty and kindness. Ataraxia could only sit in awe, feeling as though she was witnessing something rare and precious-Cherish was not just a girl, she was a perfect harmony of nature's most delicate and powerful touches.

Everything about her was a contradiction. Delicate but strong. Silent but expressive. Close yet impossibly distant.

**Cherish isn't just a girl—she's the kind you rarely come across in a lifetime.**

The first time I saw her, I didn't feel much. But today, I realize she's flawless. Everything about her is simply perfect her nature, her behavior, the way she carries herself. She is the original. No one can match her, let alone imitate her. Copies may exist, but the original remains unmatched and she is that masterpiece.

She's the kind of person you can't help but fall for. Her eyes alone could make the world pause so deep, so enchanting, that one glance is enough to leave anyone breathless. Honestly, she's like a work of art, a living painting sculpted with grace and soul.

**She's not just seen—she's felt.**

The way she talks, the softness in her silences, the laughter that lights up the quiet every little. detail about her feels like poetry written in motion. And maybe, just maybe, people like her aren't born often they're sent, once in a blue eternity.

Once you see her, you'll know you've never met anyone like her before. She's Al in everything she does. And honestly, I could say so much more, but words still wouldn't her justice

Though I can't share her picture without her permission, I do have a watercolor sketch of her eyes I once made-perhaps that will help you understand what I mean.

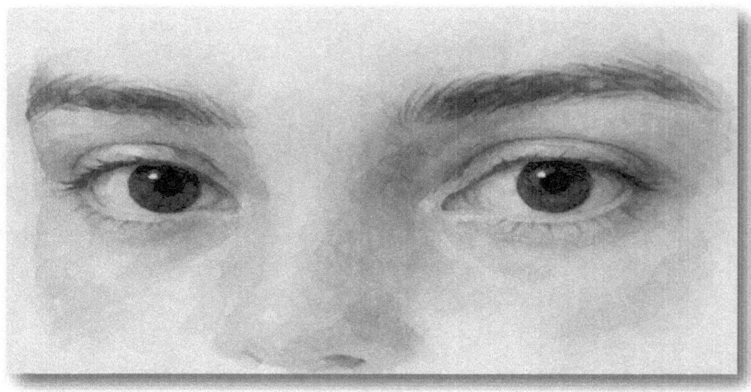

**THE UNDEFINED LINES OF ATARAXIA & CHERISH**

Make be its not perfect but Trust perfect one in the whole world ,and she is the only and only one piece in the whole Universe.

**"She didn't walk into his life; she glided into his soul."**


**<u>That's lines are truly written for her:</u>**

*"Sochta hoon tumhari khubsurti pe kuch likh doon,*
*par ruk jaata hoon... kahin padhne wala tumhara deewana na ban jaaye."*

As the day closed, Ataraxia was left with one thing: a feeling. A feeling that something had changed-not just between them, but within him.

They had finally met. But was this the beginning of something new, or the closing scene of a story that never got its ending?

**"When you finally meet the person who's lived in your thoughts for years... do they feel more like a memory or a future?"**

And now, dear reader, the café has emptied. The coffee has gone cold. But the heart still brews a hundred questions:

- **Will they meet again?**
- **Will words finally replace silence?**
- **Or will this be remembered as the last chapter they wrote together... without even knowing it?**

---

*"Puri duniya ke jazbaat ek taraf,*
*Usse wo pehle mulakat ek taraf!!*

# THE SILENCE BETWEEN THE LINES

### CHAPTER VI : THE SPACE BETWEEN REPLIES

**"Some distances are not measured in miles or meters but in missed calls, unread messages, and unspoken feelings."**

The cafe door closed behind her, but to Ataraxia, the scent of her lingered longer than the hour they spent together. Even after she had walked away, his soul remained seated, watching the space she once occupied, whispering silently: Was this a beginning or a farewell in disguise?

The first meeting the only real meeting had felt like a dream threaded in rose gold. But the morning after was a different reality. No calls. No messages. A quietness loud enough to echo through every room of his heart.

Ataraxia tried to distract himself, diving into books, listening to music, staring at the same pages of poetry he once wrote for her. Yet, her laughter, her voice, her glow they were like sun-stains on glass, impossible to wipe off.

Cherish, too, had retreated. Not out of ignorance, but intention. She had promised herself discipline this year exams loomed like heavy clouds, and her future demanded attention.
And yet, late at night, her fingers hovered over his chatbox. Typing. Erasing. Typing again.

One evening, he broke the silence.

**Ataraxia:**
"How strange na, we met after so long... and now I don't even know when I'll hear your voice again."

**Cherish (after 3 hours):**
"Life sometimes gives moments that are complete in themselves... Maybe that was ours."

The message stabbed deeper than she intended. But she didn't take it back.

Days turned into weeks. Weeks to a month. Their communication shrank into a ghost of what it used to be — a reply here, a missed call there. But the connection? It remained. As stubborn as the moon chasing the tide.

Then, one night in October, just before Diwali, Cherish messaged him.

**Cherish:**
"I read one of your poems again today... the one about me, I think."
**Ataraxia:**
"They're all about you. Even the ones that don't mention your name."

She sent a voice note. Soft. Shy. And in it, she recited something she wrote:

"The first time you looked at me, I didn't know it would echo this long. The way you said my name, it found home in the deepest corners of me.
Maybe I never said it clearly-
But the way you saw me....
That's the way I wanted to be remembered."

Ataraxia closed his eyes. That was the first time he cried silently. Not because she confessed something But because he didn't know what to do with what he still felt

The echo of Cherish's goodbye still shimmered faintly in the corners of his mind. The scent of that café lingered, like memories folded into silence. But just when the world had begun to sink. back into its routine grey something happened.

It was **27th October**, just past midnight. The clock blinked **12:02 AM** when his phone buzzed.

Cherish.
She was calling.

Ataraxia's heart leaped like it knew something he didn't. He picked it up, voice trembling but soft.

**"Happy birthday, Ataraxia..."** came her voice-gentle, sweet, like a river speaking to the moonlight.

"I have a surprise for you," she whispered.

Before he could say anything more, the call ended. Moments later, a message arrived.

And it read:
**"Happy birthday, my love. I wish you all the happiness on your special day. You are truly special to me. Your charming eyes... they were the first thing that captured my heart. Stay with me, always. I love you so much, baby!!"**

Time stopped.

Ataraxia didn't know if he was breathing. The warmth of the message wrapped around him like a blanket pulled from the heavens. His hands trembled holding the phone.

Then another message came.

**"Your eyes... no one can beat them. They're so full of life and poetry. And you... you're truly something I didn't even know I needed. I've fallen for you, Ataraxia. I've been in love with you. I was just scared... scared to say it. But I was waiting for the right moment. Tonight felt right."**

A still silence held his world. A kind of quiet that doesn't ask questions just holds meaning.

But then came the ache.

Another line followed her love:

**"But I must say this too... As much as I love you, we can't be in a relationship right now. My board exams are coming. Please wait for me. Just a little more. Let love bloom at the right time."**

And that's when his soul smiled with a sadness.

He whispered to himself, like a promise:

**"Some love stories aren't paused-they're just waiting for the perfect breath."**

**"If words could speak beauty, they would call themselves his eyes."**

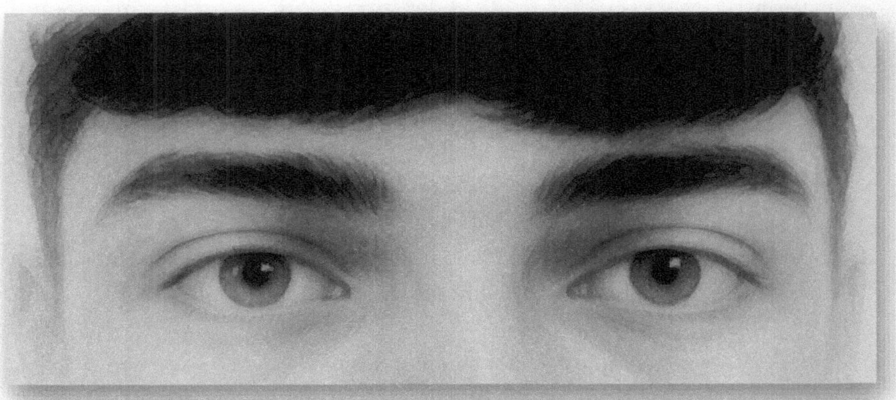

<u>**Its not perfect but the eves are thes only brown vellow!!**</u>

After that night, Ataraxia didn't need stars.

He had her voice.
He had that message.
He had hope-wrapped in the most romantic heartbreak one could receive.

**THE UNDEFINED LINES OF ATARAXIA & CHERISH**

**"It's easy to hold hands,
Harder to hold silence.
Easiest to fall in love,
Hardest to fall out."**

They began talking again, but cautiously like two dancers afraid of missteps. The late-night chats resumed. Not daily, but frequent. No longer playful, but real. Deeper.

Cherish talked about her fears, her pressure, the guilt of being unable to balance dreams and feelings. Ataraxia listened. Always.

Then one day she said,

**"Can I ask you something?"**
He replied, **"Always."**

**"Do you think... we would've lasted... if things were different?"**

Ataraxia waited before replying.

**"I think we're still lasting. Just in a way only we understand."**

They didn't label what they had. They couldn't. Maybe they were friends. Maybe more. Maybe. something that lived in the undefined lines of life.

But as the year-end approached, so did decisions. Cherish's exams were near. Her replies became slower again. Ataraxia feared another goodbye.

And just before the New Year, he sent her a message not asking for love, or clarity.

Just one thing:
**"When this is all over—
If you remember me,
Will you come back?
Even if it's just for one coffee?"**

She saw the message.

She didn't reply
Not that day.
Not for many days.
.

.

**"Maybe some stories are paused, not ended.**
**Maybe the silence isn't empty it's waiting to be filled."**

**To Be Continued...**

- **Will Cherish return after the storm of exams ends?**
- **Will Ataraxia wait, or will time write a new story in his heart?**
- **What remains when words fade memory, or longing?**

**THE UNDEFINED LINES OF ATARAXIA & CHERISH**

# CHAPTER 7
# Where Distance Wrote Us Closer

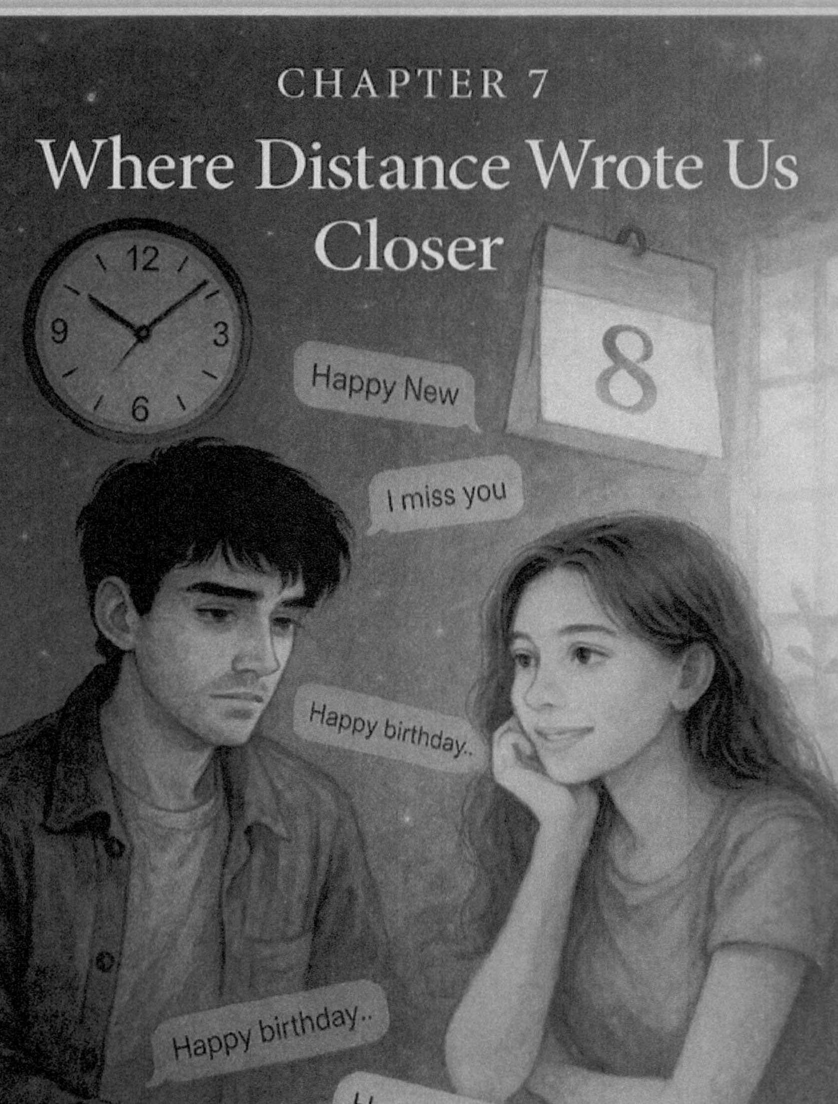

# WHERE DISTANCE WROTE US CLOSERS

### CHAPTER VII : LETTERS BETWEEN THE LINES

The silence that followed wasn't cruel.
It was agreed upon an unspoken truce carved in love and duty.

The night after Cherish's birthday message still echoed in Ataraxia's chest like a soft bell. But just as suddenly as it had come, silence returned to them-not the bitter kind, but the silence made of promises waiting patiently in the wings.

They had decided to pause to place their love in a quiet corner of time while exams loomed. And so they stopped talking, not out of anger, but out of silent agreement.

Yet in that stillness, they both missed each other desperately.

Ataraxia would stare at his books, reading the same lines twice and thrice, only to find her name floating in the white spaces. He wondered if Cherish thought of him too. If her nights ever whispered his name. If after her exams ended, she would return to him as his love-or as a stranger once again.

**"The hardest part of loving someone deeply is pretending you don't miss them when you're letting them grow."**

New Year's Eve arrived with soft snowflakes of emotion. At 12:01 AM, a message blinked on Ataraxia's screen. A quiet message blinked into their screens.

"Happy New Year."

No emojis.
No hearts.
Just polite hope.

On **6th January**, it marked **one whole year** since their first conversation. Yet, neither of them acknowledged it out loud. Some anniversaries are too delicate to touch.

February arrived—**Valentine's week**. But there were no roses, no greetings. Not because they didn't care.

But because each thought:

*"Maybe she's busy."*
*"Maybe he's studying."*
*"Maybe it's not the right time."*

A lot of girls noticed Ataraxia. But none caught his gaze.
He didn't entertain friendships, let alone feelings..

His heart, quite honestly, had already made its home in another city-inside a girl whose absence was louder than presence.

Cherish, too, was approached.
Boys tried, some even waited but she had already fallen for someone who spoke through silence and remembered her laughter by heart.

**"Loyalty isn't tested when others are around. It's tested when silence grows long and temptation knocks."**

March arrived, and with it-her board exams. Ataraxia sent a message before every paper And every exam day, without fail, Ataraxia would send her a quiet blessing:

**"You've got this. Just write like the stars are watching you."**

*"Best of luck, genius. You'll do wonders. I believe in you."*

And after every test, she would just send a small:
**"Thank you."**

And finally, on **2nd April**, her last paper was over.

That evening, the silence broke.

Their messages began to flow again, at first like tiny ripples-simple, soft, careful. But after April 15th, once Ataraxia's own school exams ended, it was as if the dam burst. And this time, it was different.

They called.

They laughed.

They roasted each other with sharp wit and playful jabs.

*"Are you sure you passed?"*
*"With your luck, I bet your pen gave up before you did."*

They talked for hours-on calls, on chats, with laughter and longing dancing in their words. They teased. They roasted each other. They shared secrets like childhood friends. And they turned their bond into something warm and spicy-because Cherish loved that twist.

Cherish liked to spice up conversations.
She turned their healthy bond into a playful storm.

And Ataraxia?

He welcomed it with open arms.

*Some relationships don't need a label-they bloom wild, beautiful, and just enough to become a world of their own."*

They said goodbye a thousand times.
But never once did they mean it.

**"Some bonds aren't defined by relationship status.
They're defined by how quickly you miss someone the moment they go silent."**

Their bond was like music with no end note. Where other relationships required constant check-ins, theirs breathed in space and trust. Cherish shared her schedule only when she wanted to. Ataraxia never asked. He didn't need to.

They weren't possessive.
They didn't need to ask each other's every move.
They trusted.

If Cherish wanted to share her day—she did.
If not, Ataraxia never asked.

They fought, sometimes. Every fight would last no longer than a few hours. Silence would settle for a moment, but always, always they returned stronger, deeper, softer.

But their longest silence lasted only two Days.
Maybe three.

**"In a world that rushes love, they chose to build it slow-so it never fell apart."**

Summer vacations ended. Results came. Cherish had aced her boards-**A1 grade**. Ataraxia was proud in the quietest, most thunderous way. She took admission in another city, pursuing competitive exam preparation.

Ataraxia moved up a grade as well.
Now it was his turn to face board exams. And again, the winds of distance crept in.

And so, life rotated again.
The intensity of love simmered into soft rituals-short chats, long silences, and quiet hope.

On **23rd May**, Ataraxia poured his heart into a beautiful message:

*"To the girl who paused time and painted my life with meaning–Happy Birthday. You are more than special. You're the poetry the universe forgot to write until it saw you smile."*

He planned a small party, a virtual one–cake, wishes, music she loved.

But Cherish was too busy.

*"I'm really sorry, love. I wish I could've been there."*

He smiled.
Not with his lips. But with his patience.

**"Loving someone means showing up for them... even when they can't show up for you."**

June melted into July.
July danced into August.

And then, **September arrived.**

On the **8th of September**, Ataraxia's phone rang.

The screen blinked.

**Cherish Calling...**

He stared at it.
Heart racing.
Fingers trembling.

Because something in that moment whispered...

*"After this call, nothing will be the same."*
**"Some silences break not with words, but with storms."**

## "Dooriyon Ke Darmiyaan"

*Tere bina bhi jee liya maine,*
*Par har raat ne tera naam liya maine.*
*Khamoshiyon mein teri awaaz thi,*
*Pal pal mein teri hi saaz thi.*

*Din dhalte socha tujhe,*
*Shaam ke jhonke mein mehsoos kiya tujhe.*
*Phone ke screen pe naam tera na tha,*
*Par dil ka wallpaper bas tera tha.*

*Waqt tha par baat nahi hoti thi,*
*Baat hoti thi par aankhon se nahi hoti thi.*
*Tu khud mein uljhe the, main bhi khud mein gum,*
*Phir bhi dil keh raha tha — "kab miloge tum?"*

*Valentine bhi aaya, bina ishare ke gaya,*
*Par dil ne phir bhi tujhe hi chaha, na shikayat kiya.*
*Naye log aaye, naye chehre dikhe,*
*Par tu jaisa koi na mila, yeh dil ne Kaha.*

*Har exam ke din tujhe duaon mein rakh liya,*
*Aur har result ke din tujhe yaadon mein chhupa liya.*
*Tere "Good luck" ke shabd, mere taweez ban gaye,*
*Teri har baat, meri duaon ke saath chal gaye.*

*Tere birthday pe waqt na tha,*
*Phir bhi har pal mein tera zikr tha.*
*Tera naam le kar chaand ko dekha,*
*Us roshni mein tera chehra socha.*

*Hamari kahani mein zyada milna nahi tha,*
*Par zyada sochna, har pal ka nasha tha.*
*Rishton ki paribhasha se pare,*
*Hum dono ek duje ke liye thai.*

*Tu batati nahi sab kuch,*
*Par mujhe sab samajh aata tha.*
*Main bhi chup tha,*
*Par har khamoshi teri yaadon ka paighaam laata tha.*

*Door the par juda kabhi nahi hue,*
*Har doori mein kuch aur kareeb hue.*
*Log kahte hain waqt sab kuch mita deta hai,*
*Par yeh toh humein aur likh gaya — naye Lafzo mein, naye jazbaat ke saath.*

*Jab tu aaye call pe 8 September ki shaam,*
*Dil ne kaha — kahani ab bhi hai adhoori, par intezaar hai aaj bhi.*

---

- **What did Cherish say on that call?**
- **Did the silence finally bloom... or break?**

THE UNDEFINED LINES OF ATARAXIA & CHERISH

# When You Left, You Took the Noise — But Left the Echo

# THE GOODBYE THAT LEFT THE DOOR OPEN

### CHAPTER VIII : THE EXIT THAT WAITED

*["Sometimes, silence isn't distance... it's the last string of hope playing its tune."]*

**8 September 2022—10:11 PM**

Ataraxia's phone lit up in the soft darkness. The name flashing on the screen was one he hadn't seen or heard from in what felt like entire seasons passing — **Cherish.**

His heart pounded like a forgotten melody rediscovering its rhythm. His hands trembled like a violin string touched by a gentle breeze. He swiped up.

**"Hello?"**

There was a pause. Then came the voice. Familiar. Fragile. Faintly broken

**"Are you free?"**

**"Yes... always for you,"** he replied, his voice low, hesitant, but filled with the warmth only she had ever drawn out of him.

Silence.
And then, her words fell like glass shattering:

"I'm sorry... this can't work anymore. I want to end everything."

Before he could even form a word, she continued

"No explanations, no reasons... Just I'm sorry. Goodbye."

*Click*.

The call ended.
And something inside him did too.

That night, Ataraxia didn't shed a single tear. Not because he wasn't hurting but because the hurt was too deep for tears. Like a wave crashing inward.

He didn't call her back. Didn't text. Didn't question. He lay on his bed, eyes open, staring into a ceiling that had suddenly become too heavy to bear. Sleep found him not as peace, but as escape.

---

The Next Morning - 9 September 2022

He reached for his phone.

**Blocked.**

On everything.
Everywhere.

Panic came first. Then confusion. Then silence again. He tried renching out. Once Twice Ten times. Then stopped.

He told himself- *She must be overwhelmed. Her studies. Her future. Maybe I became a distraction.*

But doubts bred in the shadows.

**Was she okay?**

**Did someone else come into her life?**

**Did he fail to understand her?**

<u>**Questions—endless. Answers—none.**</u>

Overthinking wrapped itself around his mind like a blanket stitched from invisible threads. He deleted his social media. Closed off. Isolated.

**Every day: school — home — books — overthinking — sleep. Repeat.**
And then—late one night—unable to bear the silence, he poured his ache into words:

---

### <u>Tum Bina Kaise Guzar Gaya Har Din</u>

*Tum gayi toh kuch bhi saath na raha,*

*Na hasi, na neend, na raasta.*

*Har pal mein tera zikr tha, Khud se chhup chhup ke ro liya maine har dafa.*

*Khaamoshi bhi aaj kal cheekhti hai,*

*Aur yaadein raat bhar jhaankti hai. Jo keh na sake tum, vo har lafz ban gaya,*

*Tum door ho kar bhi mere paas ban gaya.*

---

**October 2022- The Weight of Memory**

As the days crawled into October, the ache didn't lessen it deepened.

Autumn arrived, and with it, falling leaves reminded Ataraxia of falling conversations one by one, they disappeared, until there was nothing but empty branches.

He'd walk home through quiet lanes, hoping to spot a reminder of her. A song she loved playing in a shop. A girl who looked like her passing by. A message. A sign.

**THE UNDEFINED LINES OF ATARAXIA & CHERISH**

But there was only the silence.

But in the silence he feels that he lost everything; there is nothing remaining as he thinks only of just one hope, that she will come back, but inwardly he feels like...

*Kabhi aisa hua hai ki har kisi cheez se bas mann sa uth gaya ho? Aajkal pata nahi kyun mujhe aisa lag raha hai. Kuch pasand nahi aa raha. Aur ab to is baat se udaas hoon ki udaas kyun hoon, uski wajah bhi nahi pata. Log gawaata gaya hoon main. Baat karne ke liye bhi aisa koi nahi hai kareeb. Jo kaam pasand tha mujhe, ab woh bhi dara raha hai. Mujhse door hone lagi hai meri har pyaari cheez. Main har kaam jhat se karne waala, aaj thak kaise sakta hoon? Mujhe koi bhi cheez khush kyun nahi kar rahi hai? Main hanske rehne waala insaan aisa ban kaise sakta hoon? Kahin mann na lage to aam baat hai na. Par agar mann hi uth jaaye, tab kya karte hain?*

---

**27 October 2022-Just Two Days Before His Birthday**

He still held onto hope.

If she hasn't truly forgotten, she'll wish me at 12:00 AM.

The clock ticked.

11:59...
12:00...
12:01...

Everyone else wished.
But not her.

The silence became unbearable.

So he did what his heart always turned to he wrote:

<h1 style="text-align:center"><u>Main Tera Intezaar Karta Raha</u></h1>

Raat ke barah baje, saari duniya mere saath thi,

Par jiske ek lafz ka intezaar tha, wo khamosh thi.

Tere bina yeh birthday adhoora sa laga,

Tere bina har pal bejaan sa laga.

Dil samjha, tu busy hogi kahin,

Par aankhon ne toh bas tera raasta dekha yahin par.

**12:23 PM — The Call**

His phone rang. Again, her name. Again, his breath froze.

She spoke softly: **"Happy Birthday, Ataraxia."**

He half-laughed, half-cried.

**"I'm such a fool, na?** I waited the whole night, thinking you'd call at midnight."

She smiled. He could hear it.

**"12 AM or 12 PM... just numbers. But I remembered, didn't I?"**

It was short. Sweet, Painful. Hopeful.

They hung up.

And he stared at the ceiling again this time, with a soft smile.

***She remembered............***

As a type of Birthday wish he want he didn't get so some what he realise one thing that as he do the love he didn't get it im the same way as he given to her so Perceive that;



---

**November-December 2022- The Silent Season**

They didn't speak

But they thought of each other daily.

She was buried in entrance exam preparation. He was swallowed by board exam pressure.

**Messages stayed unsent. Words unspoken. Feelings? Unchanged.**

Each night, their minds whispered: Maybe today? Maybe tomorrow? But no one broke the silence.

The winter felt colder than ever. Not because of the weather, but because of the absence.

**He would see her old messages, still saved. A shared photo. An audio note. He played it once—just to hear her laugh. He didn't sleep that night.**

---

1 January 2023- A New Year Begins

He messaged her: **"Happy New Year."**

She saw it nine hours later.

**No reply.**

But at 7 PM another call.

**"Happy New Year," she said gently. "And... this year is your board exam. Please don't text or call me. Just focus."**

Before he could respond, the line disconnected,

This time, his chest felt tighter. Not from heartbreak but finality.

**"Maybe she's found someone new... maybe I'm just a fading chapter in her story,"** he thought.

He closed his eyes. Inhaled deeply.

And dove into his books—not out of motivation–but distraction.

---

**January to February to March–Isolation in Motion**

He became a ghost to the world..

No music. No messages. No memories aloud.

But deep within, her name echoed a silent hymn.

He studied. He focused.
He obeyed her last words like a promise.

His board exams began: **2 March 2023.**

He hoped she'd wish him luck.

**She didn't.**

Now one hope remained:

"After my last exam... maybe then."

But it say's na,

*Cheezein kahan khubsurat hoti hain,*

*Khubsurat to lamhe yaadein aur kuch log hote hain.*

---

27 March 2023-The Last Paper

He stepped out of the exam hall exhausted, relieved, unsure.

His eyes scanned the crowd. His fingers checked his phone.

**Nothing.**

He looked at the sky.

**"Will she call? Or was this truly—the end?"**

He didn't know,

**But hope? Still flickered.**

And so, another poem was born. one the world would read... or maybe, just her.

---

## "*Doorivon Ke Darmiyaan*"

*Tere jaane ke baad, har din ek kahaani sa ban gaya,*

*Main likhta gaya, tu mehsoos hoti gayi.*

*Main tha page, tu thi roshni,*

*Main tha tanha, tu thi kahin door magar saath si.*

*Jab duniya ne kaha, sab khatam ho gaya,*

*Mera dil kehta raha vo aayegi kabhi wapas.*

*Ab yeh intezaar bhi mera raaz ban gaya hai,*

*Jo sirf lafzon mein jhalakta hai, tere naam ke saath.*

**To Be Continued...**

**"When goodbyes don't come with answers, hearts start writing their own."**

THE UNDEFINED LINES OF ATARAXIA & CHERISH

# Chapter 9:
## The Undefined Line of Ataraxia & Cherish
## The Day I Held Her Hand

# THE DAY
# I HELD HER
# HAND

## CHAPTER IX : THE WARMTH OF HER HAND

["Sometimes, it's not the silence that breaks us it's the echoes we wait for."]

**28 March 2023- The Day After the Final Exam**

The day rolled in with the kind of emptiness that only unfulfilled hope brings.

Ataraxia had waited... and waited.
But **there was no message.**
No call.
No sign.

Not even a whisper through the digital wind. And in that stillness, grief took root a strange kind. Not the grief of someone's death, but the grief of someone still alive who's no longer with you

## *Grief-A Feeling Without Language*

*"Grief ek aisa emotion hota hai jo akele insaan ko andar se kha jaata hai. Jab tum kisi ko poori dil se chahte ho, aur voh bina kisi wajah ke door chala jaye... voh feeling-vohi grief hoti hai.*

*Kabhi kabhi, yeh grief aankhon se aansu ban kar girta hai. Kabhi kabhi, bas ek lambe saans ki tarah ruk jaata hai. Aur kabhi kabhi... yeh bas likh jaata hai, kisi diary mein, kisi line mein, kisi text ke beech.*

*Ataraxia ke liye, voh grief ek din ya ek moment nahi tha voh har pal tha jab usne apne phone ko dekha... aur kuch nahi mila.*

*Vo har din, har ghadi uska dil sirf yeh puchta raha: "Kya mai bhool gaya jaane layak tha?"*

---

**29 March 2023-8:00 PM**

That night, Ataraxia was having dinner with his family. His phone lay silently on the table beside his plate.

Suddenly-
**A notification sound buzzed.**
A different tone. Something custom. Something familiar.
He froze.

The screen lit up.

**Cherish.**

She had messaged.
Three words simple, explosive.

**"Heyy, are you forgotten me?"**

His heart skipped. Then raced. His fingers shook.
He wiped them on his jeans and typed quickly:

"No. Never."

---

The Chat Continued:

**Cherish**: "So... how was your last paper?"

**Ataraxia**: "It went well... but not as well as it would've if you were there."

A pause.

**Ataraxia**: "Can we talk? Like really talk like we used to?"

**Cherish**: "I don't think now is the right time... I'm sorry."

Ataraxia's heart sank a little. But he wasn't ready to give up. He had waited months for this window. He pleaded gently.

**"Please... can we meet? Just once? Not to argue, not to fight... just to talk. One time."**

She took time.

Then the reply came:

**"Okay. I want to meet too. I have something to tell you."**

They fixed the date.

2nd April, Saturday
7 PM
A meeting. A moment. A possibility.

---

## The Wait That Broke the Clock

From 29 March to 2 April, Ataraxia lived inside a mind loop.

*"Is this the last time we'll meet?"*
*"Will she tell me it's over forever?"*
*"Or... will she tell me about someone new?"*
*"Maybe... maybe we'll find a way back."*

He rehearsed what he'd say. Imagined her smile. Practiced being calm.

But one thought—kept hammering:
**"Please, let me just see her once."**

---

## 2 April 2023- The Day of the Meeting

He dressed carefully plain but neat. Hair combed. Shoes clean. A faint perfume. His heart pounded with each second. And just before stepping out, he turned around and entered the small prayer room in the house.

The boy who didn't pray even before exams—now **stood folded hands before God,**

> *"Yaar, maine tujhse kabhi kuch nahi manga.*
> *Sirf ek cheez... ek insaan mang raha hoon.*
> *Agar usse mil jaane ka mauka de raha hai...*
> *toh please kuch accha hi karna.*
> *Bas ek baar... dekh to loon usse."*

His family watched from afar—stunned.
The boy who never folded hands—today, was almost begging.

---

## 6:50 PM-At the Meeting Spot

Ataraxia reached the meeting point. Nervous, pacing. He took out his phone to call her. But just before he could—
**A new message appeared.**

"Hey... sorry. I'm busy today. Can't meet. We'll have to cancel."

Everything inside him crumbled.

He dialed.
No answer.
He waited 5 minutes. She finally called back.

Ataraxia (softly): "I'm here... I didn't read the message earlier. I'm waiting."

Cherish: "I know, but I really can't today. I'm caught up."

Ataraxia: "Please... just 5 minutes. I came only for you."

Cherish: "Give me 2 minutes. I'll call you."

Two longest minutes of his life later...

Cherish: "Okay, come pick me up."

## The Meet: A Silence Full of Words

He picked her up.

They didn't know where to go.

They roamed for a while, confused and quiet, till they found a café that felt just right - small, dimly lit, tucked away from noise.

They sat.

**Cherish:** "I know I disappeared. I'm sorry."

They sat together in silence at first—
a quiet only broken by the weight of unspoken words.

They sat together in silence at first-a quiet only broken by the weight of unspoken words.

Then, Cherish turned to Ataraxia, her voice trembling with both curiosity and hidden pain.

"So... what's going on in your life?"
She asked, trying to smile.

"Are you thinking that I've moved on?
That I made a new friend, and now... I've forgotten you? That I'm happy without you?"

Ataraxia didn't say a word. He just looked at her, quietly listening, his silence echoing louder than any answer.

And then, her voice cracked-soft, raw, and aching.

"Sorry, yaar... I shouldn't have left your life like that, without saying anything. But there were so many problems in my life... I couldn't understand anything. I was lost. That's why I disappeared..."

She paused, wiping the corner of her eye.

"But even today-I love you. Even today-I want you. I was only waiting for your board exams to end. I was going to message you after that... but then I thought, maybe you've forgotten me. Maybe you moved on. And that thought... it killed me."

Ataraxia's heart ached. He had waited so long for this moment, and now her voice was trembling, drenched in love and regret.

"I never thought like that," he said softly. "Not even once. Every day, I waited. I just believed you'd come back. I kept holding onto that hope."

Both of them sat there, the wounds between them visible like stars on a clear night-far apart, yet still part of the same sky.

We both faced problems in life," he continued gently, "but even through it all... I never forgot you. I couldn't."

Then, his voice turned into a question-soft, yet piercing. "But why didn't you tell me? Why did you leave without a single word?"

Cherish could no longer hold back the tears. She looked down and spoke in a broken whisper:

"It made me feel so insecure...
I felt pathetic.
I questioned my worth every night
I convinced myself I wasn't someone worth loving..."

Ataraxia had no words. Her pain was too deep, too real. He could only feel it-a storm crashing inside her, and now inside him.

Then, with eyes full of emotion, Cherish looked at him and asked the question she'd buried for months:

"How could you give up so easily?
How did you not find a reason to stay?
I was so tired... fighting alone."

Her words pierced through him  soft and sharp as glass. Ataraxia's chest tightened as he watched her, and something inside him broke open.

He leaned in gently and said, his voice low and sincere, "Cherish... can I touch your hand?"

She nodded quietly.

Their fingers met like old promises reuniting-her hand slipped into his, trembling slightly at first, then gripping tightly, as though letting go might mean losing everything again.

Ataraxia held her hand with both of his, looking into her eyes.

"Don't worry," he whispered.
"I'm here now. And I promise-I'll never leave you again. No matter what comes, no matter how dark it gets... I'm not going anywhere."

And for the first time in a long time, their silence didn't feel empty.

It felt like home.

**Ataraxia: "Do you know how many stories I told myself while you were gone?"**

**She chuckled.**

**"Tell me."**

He opened up. His overthinking, his pain, the poems he wrote.

---

**Cherish asked, curious:**

**"Why didn't you just move on?"**

**Why you love me today also?**

**Why you care for me?**

**What I mean to you?**

Ataraxia: Back then, I had no answers to any of your questions. I was lost-unsure of what to say, or even what I was feeling. But now... now, I hold the answers to all your questions.

Now, I Junderstand what my silence meant, and what your words truly carried..

SO THE ANS IS HER:

**1. Why didn't you just move on?**

>> You are the sunshine that brightens my mornings and the stars that gently light up my nights. Moments like these tender, rare, and unforgettable-will forever live in the quiet corners of my heart, because you are truly special to me. Your smile lingers in my memories like the scent of a favorite season, your laughter still echoes in my soul, and your love so deep, so real-is etched into every heartbeat I carry.

I'll never forget how much I need you, and I'll always hold close the memories we've created together. From those late-night 3 a.m. conversations to the silly jokes only we understood, every moment with you felt like a beautifully wrapped gift from time. I'll miss our spontaneous adventures, our long, heartfelt talks, and the calm silence we shared when no words were needed. I'll miss the way you made me laugh without effort, the way you challenged me to be a better version of myself, and the way you always knew how to bring light when everything felt dark.

Even though I'll miss you more than I can ever say, knowing that you're happy and successful brings me peace. You're the rhythm that makes my heart sing, the invisible thread tying me to something greater, something lasting. No matter where life takes us, I'll carry you with me-in thoughts, in dreams, in quiet moments when the world slows down and my heart remembers yours.

You are the melody that fills my soul, and even if distance places miles between us, I'll keep singing our song. I love you more than words can express, and no matter how far we are, you will remain forever and always in the embrace of my heart.


### 2. Why you love me today also?

>> I have seen me in your eves.

I have felt that love for me in your heart.

Your beats can express your love for me which your words can't.

Your smile makes my day more prettier than yesterday.

Your one text changes my mood in seconds.

The way you look at me, makes me blush.

The way you call me Babe make me feels like I'm all yours Always And Forever.

### 3. Why you care for me?

>> I care about you. If I fight with you, if I get angry on you when you don't share things with me it does make me upset. It does make me feel that you don't trust me or you don't feel safe to tell me whenever something's bothering you and you just say"I won't understand you". Yes maybe I can't always understand you but atleast you can share with me,I maybe not the best person you will ever feel to share everything but it bothers me whenever I see you sad. And maybe you won't understand but it hurts when you hide. things, it hurts when I think I am an important person to you but then you act like I am just an ordinary person. Yes sometimes I just wanna know if you trust me or not, if you feel better sharing everything with me, if I am an important person to you. But then, if I force you to share something I am sorry, I know you get angry, you just walk away you feel like I am irritating you, but I just hope you understand the reason behind it. And everytime our fights happen & you always say "Leave me alone" let me tell you,I wont leave you without making you smile, because we promised we will not walk away when we see each other sad, even if you are rude to me, even if we don't talk for days I know you will send me a text, make me a call & tell me "How you acted differently, and you are all sorry about it" & like everytime I will always be there for you, I will not be the one giving up Just understand that I care about you a lot, & if I question you, texts you a numbers of times when I feel somethings wrong do not get irritated because you know when you are much more important to me than I can explain.....

### 4. What I mean to you?

>> **YOU MEAN EVERTHING TO ME:** *Everytime you ask me "What YOU mean to you" Right. Listen, remember the first time we met, we were strangers, we didn't even actually knew anything about each other..*

*But today if they ask me what the relationship 1 share with you.I would just say "I am blessed to have a person like you in my life". Maybe we weren't comfortable much before but in the recent months when I talk with you, I feel better, I feel I have someone who understands me.I don't share everything with people 1 meet people who said they care about me left.people who said "I like the way you are" judged me when I acted weird. But then I found you. A weird person who always loved me.cared for me and no matter what I did, how rude I am always knew how to handle my moods. From "Can I tell you something"? to "Hey, Tell me what happened" you always were with me.Sorry for being too possesive over you, its like when you ignore me I have a feeling of being replaced that's the only reason I am rude sometimes when I see you with someone else I wonder if you will stop talking to me. Will I lose my 2am partner who always listened to my talks,never complained about how much I overreact at times.cried with me, made me laugh.hugged me tight when no one was there for me. It's because I am so close to you that I cant think of losing you. If you get tired of me someday, just tell me, but please don't ever leave me.I don't want anyone else, I just want you. Dont reply me in minutes, dont talk on calls for hours but just promise me one thing "Just dont ignore me for someone else, Just dont replace me". Please.I just dont want to again lose a special person in my life.*

**THESE ALL ARE THE ANSWERS FOR CHERISH QUESTIONS..**

---

## The Touch That Meant Everything

A pause came. A gentle silence.

Then, Ataraxia whispered:

"Can I... hold your hand?"

**Cherish (smiling):** "Yes. Why not?"

He reached out—held her hand.

"Don't worry. I'm here now. And I won't leave."

She looked at him, almost in awe.

*"Seriously... you're something else. You're the only boy I know who asks before touching.*
*Aaj kal koi takra jaye toh sorry bhi nahi bolta.*
*Tum... you're rare."*

## The Future Still Unclear

**Cherish:** "But I still have my entrance exams. I can't handle love and studies both. If you think it's easy, prepare once yourself you'll know."

Ataraxia didn't argue.

He nodded.

"Maybe I can't understand completely... but I can wait. Just don't shut the door."

**9:43 PM On The Way Home**

He dropped her home.

On the way back, he rode slowly. Each streetlight casting long shadows on his mind.

*"What was this?*
*A new beginning?*
*Or a goodbye wrapped in soft words?"*

# "Tum Aayi, Toh Sawal Saath Aaye"

Tum aayi, toh ek khushi si lagi,
Par har muskurahat ke peeche, ek wajah chhupi lagi.

Yeh haath toh thaam liya tumne,
Par kya yeh haath chhoc dogi kal, yeh darr bhi tha saath mein.

Main kuch poochh nahi saka,
Kyuki jawab tumhare aankhon mein the aur main darr gaya.

---

*"Some meetings are not about answers they're about keeping hope alive... long enough to matter."*

**THE UNDEFINED LINES OF ATARAXIA & CHERISH**

# THE YEARS WE PROMISED, THE SILENCE WE BORROWED

## CHAPTER X : A SHIFT IN THE AIR

That evening, just after reaching home, the phone rang.

Her name on the screen Cherish calling was enough to melt the chaos within him. Ataraxia. picked up the call, and before he could even say hello, she softly asked. "Reached safely?"

That one question—simple, but laced with care—made something inside him sigh. And for the next hour, they talked,

They talked like nothing had ever broken between them. Laughter tiptoed into the conversation. Pauses turned into poetry. Even silence felt like it held hands with memories.

---

**"Kuch rishtay aise hote hain, jo sirf lamhon mein nahi, sanson mein jeete hain."**
(Some bonds don't live in moments, they live in breath.)

---

As the call ended, Ataraxia stared at the ceiling of his room. Something heavy ached in his chest.

**Regret.**

Not because of what happened. But for what he had thought.

He whispered to himself, "Kaash maine uske baare mein itna negative nahi socha hota..."

He remembered how his thoughts had turned cruel assuming she had moved on, left him, forgotten what they once were. But after hearing her speak, after feeling the same warmth in her voice, he realized she had never changed.

**"I just feared her silence louder than I trusted her love."**

She was always loyal. Always honest. Always *herself*.

---

**"Woh ladki sab jaisi nahi thi. Woh ek tukda thi us asmaan ka, jahan sirf sacchai aur wafadari basti hai."**
(She wasn't like the rest. She was a fragment of a sky where only truth and loyalty reside.)

---

Ataraxia sat there in silence and thought—
**"No one can ever be like her."**
No one. And maybe no one ever should.

That night, their story didn't restart with fire or storm. It resumed with **understanding**.
With the unspoken promise that this time, they would **walk slow, but walk far.**

## The Days That Followed

Three years passed like verses in a slow-moving song. Not every line rhymed, not every moment sparkled—but every beat mattered. They didn't speak daily. Just 30 to 40 minutes a day. Cherish had her studies, her dreams, and Ataraxia respected that.

*"She was never a page I could turn—she was the ink that wrote my soul."*

**Sometimes it was just:**
**"Did you eat?"**
**"How was your class?"**
**"I missed your laugh today."**

And sometimes, silence spoke for them.

---

**"Pyar har waqt baat nahi karta, kabhi kabhi sirf saath hone ka ahsaas hi kaafi hota hai."**
(Love doesn't always speak sometimes just feeling each other's presence is enough.)

---

April slipped away in study sessions and shared smiles.

Then came **May**...

On **May 23,** it was Cherish's birthday,

They couldn't be physically together, but as the clock struck twelve, Ataraxia made a video call.
He wished her with his heart dancing through his smile.
She smiled back, and in that pixelated moment, they felt closer than any two people in the same room,

**"Sometimes, the best gifts are not things but time, presence, and a soul that remembers."**

---

**"Dooriyon ka kya hai, woh toh sirf lambai napti hain... mohabbat toh nazron mein bhi mehsoos hoti hai."**
(Distances measure length, not love. Love is felt even through a glance.)

---

Then came a big milestone.
Ataraxia's board exam results.

He scored an **A1**.
Cherish was the first person he told.

She jumped with joy over the call, her voice laced with pride.
They laughed. They dreamed. They planned,

But life, as always, had its own blueprints.

## The Two-Year Decision

For further studies, Ataraxia got admission in another city. Distance expanded not just in kilometers, but in time, in routine.

On **June 3**, after a long and emotional conversation, they decided something mature
**A break for two years.**

Two years of silence.
Two years of trust.
Two years of personal growth, before they could fully return to each other.

No distractions. Just dreams.
A promise to focus, to grow—but still be theirs.

**"Love is not always in holding on. Sometimes, it's in growing apart, so we may come together better."**

**"Kabhi kabhi mohabbat ko bhi waqt ki chhutti chahiye hoti hai, taaki dono apne sapnon ke peechhe daud sakein."**
(Sometimes even love needs a pause, so both can chase their dreams.

They agreed. Maturely, Calmly.
And so began the **silent love story**.

They spoke just 1-2 times a month.
Cherish was preparing for her entrance. Ataraxia was adjusting to his new city and life.

## New People, New Lessons

In the institute, Ataraxia met someone. A senior. They talked first about studies, then life.

They laughed. They helped each other.

But soon Ataraxia realized this friendship was becoming something more.

And that scared him.

He didn't want to be unfair to **anyone** — not Cherish, not this new friend.
So he did the right thing he **ended it.**

The girl was hurt. Ataraxia was too.
But some silences are better than guilt.

After that Ataraxia found a new friend named **Eccedentesiast**, and together they formed an unbreakable bond — the kind of friendship that feels like finding a rare treasure, they sit together in class, sharing the same table, exchanging our daily study goals, and challenging each other to do better every day. This journey we share has its ups and downs, but through it all, it has become one of the best parts of his life.

Alongside Eccedentesiast, Ataraxia found a part of an amazing group of friends two boys and three girls whose names start with T, S, K, and V. We talk about studies, sure, but what truly stands out is the care and support we show each other. This group feels like a family, united not only by books but by genuine concern and laughter.

Among them, Eccedentesiast stands apart — because he knows everything about Ataraxia, the good and the bad memories. Our friendship is rare and precious. It's a moment in life I know will never come back.

He has been my guide and support in every journey, helping he even when he acts a little mischievous like a brother teasing but always there when it matters most.

Honestly, no matter what, he always gets the work done, and that's what friendship is all about. Right now, this bond is the best memory I hold close the best friends I've ever had.

They didn't know about Cherish in detail, but they sensed something — a part of him held in gentle reserve.

He told Cherish about them. No secrets. No shadows.

And she smiled. Because love, when real, does not cage. It allows you to find your own skies, while knowing someone still watches your flight.

**"Kuch log sirf dosti nahi, dua ban jaate hain."**
(Some people become not just friends, but prayers.)

July turned to August. August to September. October arrived with books, sleepless nights, and the soft rustle of autumn dreams.

Then came **October 27—Ataraxia's birthday.**

He hadn't expected anything.
He told himself he was okay with silence.
He rehearsed detachment like a speech.

But midnight struck.
And just like magic, she was there.

**Cherish called.**

A video call. A smile. A wish wrapped in love. Her face, lit softly by the screen, looked like nostalgia and hope had woven themselves into a single moment.

*"Happy Birthday," she whispered, "You were born into this world, but somehow... it made mine."*

It wasn't about the distance. It never had been. They celebrated as though they sat across the same table. He didn't need a cake. He had her voice. She didn't need a hug. She had his laughter.

That day, memory became magic.

---

Then came **November**.

**Diwali**. The festival of lights.
Ataraxia visited home.
Lamps were lit. Houses were decorated. Smiles filled the streets.

But among the lights, a shadow loomed.

Someone — a mutual friend — said something about Cherish.

Something that didn't sit well.
Something that didn't match the Cherish he knew.
Something that made the candle inside his chest flicker.

He didn't react. Not immediately.

But that night, while the sky exploded with fireworks, Ataraxia felt something inside him quietly shatter.

---

**"Kabhi kabhi, sach ya jhooth nahi todta... shak tod deta hai."**
(Sometimes it's not truth or lies that break you... it's doubt.)

---

He looked up at the stars and asked silently.
**"Kya sab waise hi hai jaise dikhta hai?"**
(Is everything really the way it seems?)

The Years We Promised,
The Silence We Borrowed

His heart whispered,

**"Ya phir kahani mein abhi kuch baaki hai..."**

(Or is the story still incomplete?)

Because sometimes, it isn't absence that hurts the most it's the fear that something changed during that silence you swore to protect.

---

## Poetry to Close

In echoes of her birthday laugh,
I found the moonlight in my chest.
But Diwali whispered in broken halves—
That even stars lie in jest.

I trusted her with all my skies,
Yet shadows know how to pretend.
Did I lose her in borrowed time?
Or was I wrong to defend?

THE UNDEFINED LINES OF ATARAXIA & CHERISH

# WHEN DISTANCE MADE US DISTANT

## CHAPTER XI : WHEN MILES MEANT MORE THAN MAPS

It had been exactly eight days since Ataraxia returned to his institute after completing his vaccination. The rhythm of campus life resumed—books, friends, lectures, and the usual chaos—but something within him remained disturbingly still.

They say silence can be loud, and some nights are heavier than wars. For Ataraxia, this was one of them.

He tried to smile with his friends, tried to laugh at old jokes, and nodded through lectures with artificial focus. But every night, precisely after 1 a.m., the mask fell off. As he lay under the dim light of his room, staring at the fan spinning above, his thoughts only circled one face-Cherish.

"Jis pe tum sab kuch haar jaate ho. Uski khamoshi bhi talvaar si chubhti hai."

He trusted her. Loved her beyond explanation. Yet the pain of feeling a gap, a space, a secret-was enough to twist his heart into knots. That burning thought: "Why didn't she tell me about her new friend? Why did she hide that from me?" kept slicing through the calm like invisible blades.

A week passed in silence.

# CHAPTER 11

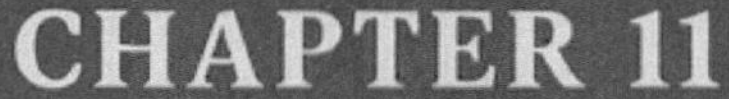

# When Distance Made Us Distant

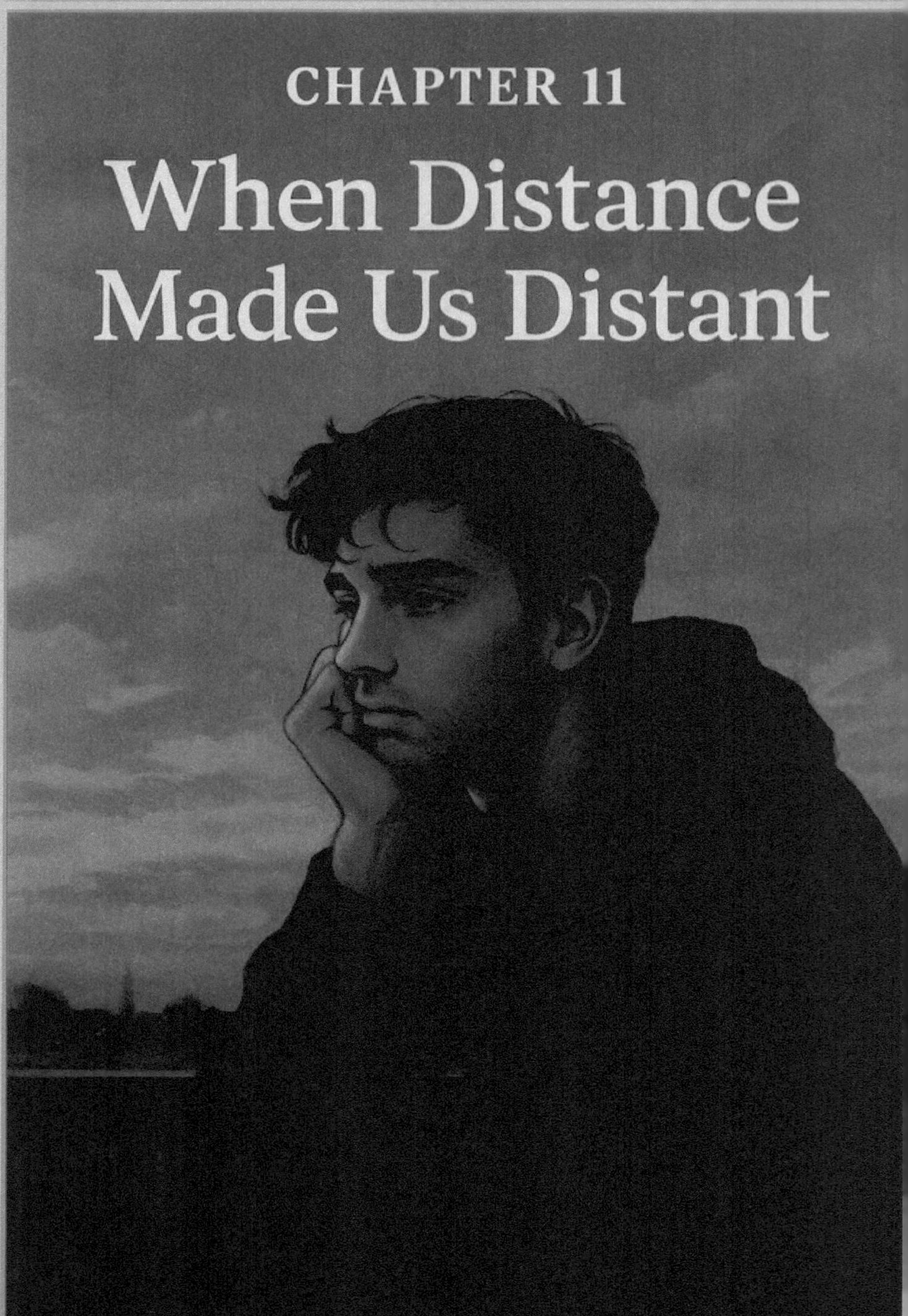

Unable to bear it anymore, Ataraxia picked up his phone and dialed her number.

**"Hey... are you busy?"**
**"No, tell me."**

And there it began.

A small question snowballed into a misunderstanding. He asked her gently, hesitantly, about her new friend. The way Cherish paused before replying told him something was already broken.

**"Yes, I made a new friend. And you didn't even trust me enough to ask before believing someone else,"** she snapped.

**"I... I didn't mean to-"**

**"I don't want to talk to you anymore, Ataraxia. Goodbye."**

The words echoed like thunder, but it wasn't the volume that shook him-it was the meaning.

She hung up.

---

**"Tere bina bhi jee lunga, ye kehna asaan tha,**
**Par tere bina jeena, khud ko har din maarna tha.**

Ataraxia waited.

One day... two... three...

But Cherish didn't call back.

He kept telling himself it was just a moment of anger, a storm that would pass. But days turned into a week. And the silence grew roots in his chest.

He tried calling. No answer.

And then came the guilt the sharpest blade of all.
*"Kya maine galat kiya? Kya space dena hi meri galti thi? Kya keh dena chahiye tha, 'Don't talk to anyone new'?"** *

But love doesn't work on boundaries. And Cherish wasn't wrong either. She only reacted to what felt like a betrayal of trust—Ataraxia believed someone else over her, even for a second.


**"Sometimes, love is not lost in storms. It's lost in the moments we hesitate to speak our heart."**

A month passed.

The world didn't pause, but Ataraxia did — emotionally.

He woke up, studied, smiled, and ate. But none of it felt real.

Yet despite the emotional tornado inside him, he didn't let his career suffer. Exams were near, and dreams waited. He worked hard. Focused. But every now and then, during late evenings or while walking alone under the yellow lights outside the hostel, her memories ambushed him.

He began writing poems. Not to impress, not to share. Just to breathe.

---

*"Raat ke 1 baje tu yaad aaye,*
*Aur aankhon ka paani chupke se muskuraye,*
*Keh na sake tujhe, lekin dil se poocha,*
*"Kya ab bhi tu mujhe yaad karti hai...?"*

---

December crept in quietly.

The air got colder, and so did Ataraxia's hope. It was nearing New Year. Everyone was making plans, setting goals, dreaming new dreams.

Except him.

He was waiting.

Still.

Somewhere deep inside, he believed Cherish would call. Maybe on the 31st. Maybe at midnight,

But what if she didn't?

What if this really was the end?

---

*"Kuch rishton ko waqt chhod deta hai, kuch ko khamoshi,*
*Aur kuch ko hum khud tod dete hain, sirf gusse mein.*
*Pata tab chalta hai, jab unki yaadon ka saath chhoot jaye."*

---

From Cherish's side, it wasn't easy either.

She was suffering. Hurt. Disappointed. She waited too, but her ego-her heartbreak-held her back. She loved him. But sometimes love stands behind pride. And unfortunately, pride rarely moves first.

She didn't make any new friends after that..

It was all a misunderstanding.

But her silence built a wall, and Ataraxia didn't know how to climb it anymore.

---

*"Ek chhoti si baat thi, jise suljha sakte the.*
*Par humne ego ke zakhm mein mohabbat dafnakar di."*

---

And still, Ataraxia waited.

Even after feeling shattered.

Even after missing her every night.

Even after knowing she may have moved on.

Because somewhere inside him, there was a boy who believed — *maybe... maybe she still loves me.*

---

**"*Wait not just with hope, but with faith —*
*That if love was true, it will find its way through silence.*"**

---

As the days ticked by, Ataraxia found himself staring more often at the sky. It was December 30. One more day to go. Maybe she'd call. Maybe she wouldn't

He picked up his diary and wrote once more.

---

**(*Final Heart Poem*):**
**"*Main ruk gaya hoon wahi, jahan tune alvida kaha tha,*
*Aaj bhi har din, wahi pal dohrata hoon,*
*Kya tu bhi kabhi wapas lautegi...?*
*Ya main sirf intezaar ki kahani ban jaunga?*"**

---

**And that's how Chapter 11 ends.**

In a cold winter night, with a boy waiting by his window, hoping the silence will finally speak. That maybe, just maybe, Cherish will return with a call, a message, a whisper that says, "I'm still yours."

But until then, the night grows deeper, and so does the wait.

---

## Sometimes, don't rush into conclusions. Don't let someone else's words decide your actions. If it's love—wait. Speak. Try. But never let silence become the goodbye you never wanted.

Will Cherish return? Or has she begun a new life journey, leaving behind the undefined line
they once walked together?

Only the next chapter will tell!!!...

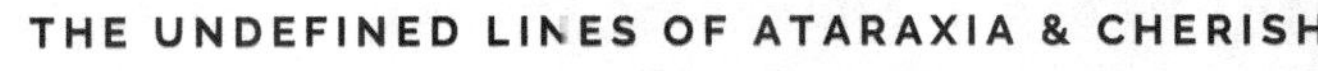

# I COULDN'T WRITE IT, THEY COULDN'T FINISH IT

## CHAPTER XII : I LEFT IT BLANK, THEY LEFT IT BROKEN

**January 1, 2025**

A new year had begun. Fireworks lit the sky. Laughter echoed through the streets. People around the world made resolutions, planned dreams, and set goals. But somewhere, in the quiet corner of his dimly lit room, Ataraxia sat silently, fingers hesitating over the keyboard of his phone

It was not just another message. It was the message.

The one where he poured his heart out. A heartfelt confession. A reflection of everything he had ever felt for Cherish. The words weren't rehearsed, just raw dripping with vulnerability, care, love, regret, and hope.

**The Message :-**

Hey

First of all, **I wish you a Happy New Year!**

I don't know how your 2024 has gone with me (in sence of talking), but from my perspective, it might not be as good as you think. I'm sorry about that. And really, thank you so much for spending another year with me. It's been four years now, and I appreciate you being by my side all this time. Thank you for

listening to everything I had to say, whether it was meaningful or not. You always listened to me, and even if what I wrote for you didn't resonate, you still encouraged me by saying you liked it. Thank you for talking with me all night, for putting in valuable effort and time for me, and a special thanks for understanding someone as crazy as me. I know I sometimes got a little angry with you, and I'm sorry for that I shouldn't have acted that way.

There's so much more to say, but I just want to express my gratitude. Everything I've written here is from my perspective. I used to think about you so much, but not everyone shares the same thoughts. Just like everyone has the same eyes, but each person's views are different.

When we look in the mirror, if we see ourselves positively, we feel good; but if we compare ourselves negatively to others, we only see our flaws and not our strengths. I used to feel that when I talk with you, I needed to reply to your messages as soon as possible, but sometimes things came up that delayed my replies. I did try, though. Whenever you said you wanted to talk, I was always eager to chat. I wanted to meet you so badly, but whenever I asked, something would come up. You would often have a genuine reason for not being able to meet, and even then, I would convince myself that we would meet eventually.

Whenever a date was set to meet, I would start preparing a week or two in advance deciding what clothes to wear, what bike to take, what to say at home, what gift to bring you, and even rehearsing lines that what to say in front of you. The only problem was that I didn't know many places, so I would ask you to choose. Sorry about that! After you picked a place, I would plan what to order, where to go for ice cream, and so much more. But it's like this: even if we got a diamond, we always want more. No matter how much you do for someone, it never feels sufficient for them.

### 'We always leave the Best one in search of Better one'

I'm really sorry if I ever made you feel that way. I genuinely enjoy spending time with you and talking to you, but I never felt that you didn't enjoy being with me or going out. I wish I had known earlier; I would have done things differently and never forced you to meet. I hope I never disrespected you in any way; I truly never meant to. But sometimes our own words can feel different to others,

and I understand if you felt hurt. I'm sorry for not meeting you more often over these four years.

I don't know why, but as I write this, tears are coming to my eyes, and I feel a bit sad. But I'm really sorry, mistakes like these won't happen again. Enjoy your life with the best people around you, and may God bless you both of you. **Thanks a lot once again for being with me as we step into 2024.**

**#Continue your story, My chapter ends here!!**

**"It takes guts to fall in love with someone"**

Just there is an one thing that I want to conve you but I know you never understand that;-

**"One of the purest thing is someone trying to fix themselves so they can love you exactly how you deserve to be loved" it's too hard..(but there is someone who still try it]**

## **Happy New year 2025**

12:10am

"I know things changed, Cherish. And maybe I wasn't enough. Maybe I misunderstood, maybe I acted out of fear... But you were always everything to me. You still are. I don't know if you'll ever read this with the heart I wrote it with, but just know: you were not just a chapter. You were the whole book."

He sent it.
And waited.

---

**A Few Days Later...**

Life has strange ways of shifting in moments. Sometimes, in the blink of an eye, everything changes. A message that could have mended something was followed by an event that shattered everything.

An incident occurred. Not just any incident-one that deeply wounded both Ataraxia and Cherish.

I wish I could explain what it was. I tried. I sat down to write their journey after that message. I wanted to tell you what happened next. But I couldn't.

**Because today is May 20, 2025**

And just earlier today, I received a phone call. It lasted only 20 minutes. But it changed everything for me.

**That call... it was about them. About Ataraxia and Cherish.**

And after listening to what I heard, I got goosebumps. My heart sank. My smile faded. My energy to write collapsed completely. My eyes filled with tears, and for the first time. I felt that perhaps some stories don't need words to end. Because they end in silence.

---

**To the Reader...**

I'm sorry.
This chapter was supposed to continue their story. But the truth is, **they couldn't complete it.** And neither could L.

It hurts when you trust someone from the deepest part of your soul and say with certainty: "**No matter what, they won't do this. I can vouch for them.**" But unfortunately, life doesn't always follow our beliefs.

When that trust shatters... it doesn't just hurt. It destroys you from within. And that's what happened. To them. To me.

I can't go into details. Not today. Not in this state. But I promise when I find strength again, I will return and tell you everything. Someday. Not as a writer. But as someone who witnessed love, hope, misunderstanding, pain, and a silent heartbreak.

---

<u>**About the Characters**</u>

Let me tell you something about Ataraxia. He destroyed himself. Not because he wanted to. But because he couldn't handle what he did. He was foolish. Impulsive. Emotional. And sometimes, emotions without understanding can become disasters. He let go of something he should have held onto tighter.

And Cherish? She's the kind of girl you won't meet twice in your lifetime. She's the masterpiece God creates only once, after years of cosmic planning. **She's flawless, graceful, deeply kind, and emotionally rare.** If you ever get a chance to meet someone like her, **know that the universe just gave you a gift beyond measure.**

Movies and books often make us crave a fictional character like **"her"**. **But Cherish was real.** And she was more beautiful, more sincere, and more perfect than fiction.

*"Kya kahun uske baare mein?*

*Har lafz kam pad jaaye,*

*har kitaab adhoori lage.*

*Vo bas ek baar milti hai zindagi mein,*

*aur jo usse paale,*

*samajh jao ki tum duniya ke sabse khushnaseeb insaan ho."*

Words fail to describe her. **Dictionaries don't contain definitions that do justice to her soul.**
And my pen... my pen simply isn't worthy.

I have a something for her.
My hands are shaking. My heart is heavy.

"Main Kitna hi thaku

Tujhse milne aane ko

Dil karta hai,


Hai kismat me nhi tu shayd...

Phir bhi ajmaane ko

Dil karta hai>>

Aur tu hai hi yesi

Ki dikhane ko zamane ko.

Dil karta hai,


Tu meri baatein sunn....

Tujhe inme uljhane ko

Dil karta hai ,

Tere julfo ke rang se rang koi

Churane ko

Dil karta hai ,

Inn Ankhon ke jaisa Mera bass

Ho jaane ko

Dil karta hai ,

Mera badal ke jaise tujhpar

Baras jaane ko

Dil karta hai ,

There are girls... and then there is Cherish.

Not a name. Not a phase. Not even a person you meet once and move on from.
Cherish is a feeling. A forever.
She's the kind of soul that makes silence speak and chaos settle.
She is not defined by beauty — she redefines it.
Not someone to admire from afar but someone so rare, even stars envy the eyes that get to see her up close.

Ataraxia once thought he understood the world.
But then came her with stardust in her eyes and galaxies hidden in her smile.
She didn't just enter his life—she rearranged his universe.

To others, she might be just a girl.
But to him...
She is the aesthetic star of the entire cosmos—
Not the kind that burns to be seen...
But the kind that exists in stillness... the kind whose presence lights up everything without trying.
No flare. No fire. Just eternal glow.
A light that doesn't need to shine to be felt.

He once tried to define her..
Tried to write about her.
But how do you capture infinity in a sentence?
How do you draw a constellation with just one star?

Ataraxia wrote a piece just a part long ago.

**THE UNDEFINED LINES OF ATARAXIA & CHERISH**

He showed her the half-written truth, and made a promise: "When I complete this... you'll be the first to hear it."

And today... that moment has come. His heart is full, his soul is calm because he has found the rest of the words. Even if they only ever express 0.1% of what she truly is, He knows that the rest cannot be written it can only be felt.

So now, as he holds his promise, with the weight of love in his breath and truth in his silence

Here is something Ataraxia wrote for Cherish:

*You are a poem as beautiful as the moon.*

*I am a blank page,*

*You are a renowned book.*

*I am just a share,*

*You are a famous ghazal.*

*I am a pile of dry leaves in autumn,*

*You are a rose blooming in the gardens.*

*I am just a black and white picture,*

*And you are a colorful art.*

*I am a burning city, You are a sky full of twinkling stars.*

*I am the autumn breeze of December,*

*And you are the warmth of the Sunshine.*

*I am like a stone lying by the river,*

*You are like a sparkling Kohinoor diamond.*

*I am one of the falling drops of rain,*

**THE UNDEFINED LINES OF ATARAXIA & CHERISH**

---

**May 20, 2025- A New Hope?**

There is one final thread left in this story. Ataraxia has decided to go back to the place where he first saw Cherish.

It's a small gathering. A little party. The date?
**May 25.**

He doesn't know if she will come. I don't know either. No one does.

But maybe, just maybe... If fate decides to take pity. If the universe feels merciful. If love still lingers...

They will meet.

One last time.

This isn't fiction. This is real. Their story. My words. Their emotions. My tears.

And for now, it remains **unfinished.**

---

# I COULDN'T WRITE IT, THEY COULDN'T FINISH IT

## PRANAY

**To My Readers:**

I'm sorry I had to cut a part of their journey after Chapter 11. I tried, I really did. But today, I am not mentally strong enough to pen it all down. That incident... it damaged something inside me too. Deeply.

But I promise you, when I feel better... When I can breathe without hurting... When I can write without crying...

**I will return. And I will finish it.**

Because some stories deserve closure. And they deserve to be remembered.

THE UNDEFINED LINES OF ATARAXIA & CHERISH

# AN UNFINISHED ENDING, A PROMISE STILL ALIVE

### THE LAST PAGE

Dear Readers.

I never thought I'd reach this page with such a heavy heart and trembling hands. I've tried-truly tried to continue Chapter 12... but something inside me just couldn't.

There are some moments in life where the pain is too personal to translate into words, where every sentence feels like reopening a wound. This chapter-this turning point in Ataraxia and Cherish's journey is one such moment.

I thought I could write it. I believed I had the strength. But today I don't.

I lost something. A part of myself, A part of them.

So, to you my dear reader-I owe honesty.

I'm sorry. I can't continue this chapter anymore.

I know you waited for closure, for answers, for that last page where everything comes together.. But the truth is, life doesn't always gift us perfect endings. Sometimes, it just leaves us with echoes and unanswered questions That's where I am. And that's where this story rests, for now.

But instead of writing further, today I want to share something more real. Something closer to the heart of this story than any perfectly crafted sentence could ever be.

I want to share with you the private notes of Ataraxia his raw, untouched thoughts that never made it into the chapters, but lived deeply within him. Maybe, just maybe, if you read them closely, you'll understand what he felt. What she meant. What was lost.

And maybe you'll find your own piece of their love hidden in between those lines.

## The 7 Stages of Love

*A Journey of Heart, Soul & Surrender*

1. **Attraction (आकर्षण)**
   The moment eyes meet, and the world pauses for a heartbeat. A spark-subtle, silent, yet powerful enough to awaken a sleeping soul.

2. **Infatuation (प्रेम-मोह / एकतरफा चाहत)**
   The illusion of love at first sight. Everything they do seems magical. You're not in love yet, but you fall... helplessly..

3. **Love (प्रेम)**
   Real, raw, and rooted. This is where the heart accepts, connects, and surrenders. It's no longer about perfection-just presence.

4. **Faith (विश्वास)**
   The invisible bond. You believe in them beyond logic, beyond distance, beyond doubt. Love grows deeper, stronger, unshakable.

5. **Worship (इबादत)**
   When love becomes sacred. You don't just love them you revere them. respect reaches its highest form, and even silence feels like prayer.

### 6. Madness (दीवानगी)

Logic fades. The heart takes full control. You laugh, cry, wait, hurt, and still love.... without reason. Obsession turns into devotion.

### 7. Death (मृत्यु)

Not always of life, but of self. The ego dies. Boundaries dissolve. In true love, the so merges so deeply, it either ends... or becomes eternal.

---

*So it's the stages of there love as in the form of checkbox :-*

## 7 Stages of Love

☑ **Attraction**
आकर्षण

☑ **Infatuation**
प्रेम-मोह / एकतरफा चाहत

☑ **Love**
प्रेम

☑ **Faith**
विश्वास

☑ **Worship**
इबादत

☑ **Madness**
दिवानगी

☐ **Death**
मृत्यु

But this is not the end.
I promise you when my heart finds peace, when my mind is no longer clouded by pain, and when I can write again with clarity and hope—**I will return.**

Yes, there will be a **Part 2**.

If there's anything left in between them if any love still breathes between Ataraxia and Cherish I will find it, and I will tell it.

And for all of you who still believe in love, in fate, in second chances...

**Here's something special:**
On May 25, Ataraxia is going live on YouTube.
In his own words, he will tell you what happened.
**Did Cherish come? Or did fate write a different end?**
You will know. Not through a page. But from his voice. His presence. His truth.

Here is the link: [https://www.youtube.com/@TheGeekyAtraxi%C3%A5](https://www.youtube.com/@TheGeekyAtraxi%C3%A5)
Watch it. Feel it. And maybe... finish it in your own hearts.

---

I leave this book **unfinished** not because it's the end—
but because some stories are too real to rush.

And like real love, they deserve time..

Thank you for walking with me this far.
Thank you for loving Ataraxia and Cherish.
Thank you for believing.

And until Part 2...
**Keep a little space in your heart for stories that pause, but never die.**

With love,
**Pranay**
— *A writer, a witness, and a believer in timeless love.*

Some stories are left
unfinished,
to make room for
new beginnings.

*Pranay*


Keep a little space in your heart
for stories that pause,
but never die.

"It's the friction of their love you can almost feel"

# ACKNOWLEDGEMENT

Before closing these pages, I want to pause not to write, but to thank. Because behind every sentence, behind every chapter, there were hearts that held me, hands that lifted me, and souls that stood silently beside me when I almost gave up.

To **Prashant Rao**,
You were not just a friend you were my mirror, my motivator, and my reminder that I could still believe in myself. When I doubted every word I wrote, you reminded me of the reason I started. Your unwavering support, honest feedback, and gentle encouragement became my fuel. Thank you for being the reason this book found its voice.

To my **family**,
From the deepest corner of my heart, I want to thank you.
To my **uncle and aunty**, and my **Bade Papa and Bade Mummy**, your blessings were like silent prayers that kept me going even when I lost strength.
To all my **siblings**, each of you added warmth to this journey. But a special part of my heart belongs to **Akshay Daa** you were more than a brother. You became my shield, my guide, my strength. I never realized how lucky I was to have someone who treats me like their own.someone who never let me fall. You are a blessing beyond words.

And to the two most important pillars of my existence—**Mummy and Papa**,
Thank you for giving me life, and then giving me the courage to live it fully. You taught me patience, love, and resilience. Every word I write, every story I dream, carries a part of your heart in it.

To my incredible **team**,
This wouldn't have been possible without you. From brainstorming ideas, to designing, to encouraging me at every setback you all are the silent heroes behind the curtains. Thank you for believing in me even when I didn't.

Lastly, to **everyone who reads these words,**
This story may have paused here, but your support has planted the seed for Part Two. I promise when healing finds me, when strength returns—I'll come back to finish what began with so much love..

Until then, thank you for walking beside me through this unfinished, yet unforgettable journey.

This book was not just a collection of chapters—it was a journey of emotions, a path carved through love, silence, regret, and hope..

First and foremost, I bow my heart in gratitude to **Ataraxia and Cherish**—not just characters, but souls who lived within every word I wrote. Thank you for teaching us that sometimes love isn't perfect, but it's always real. You both became a part of me in a way I never imagined. Even if your story is left unfinished for now, it's engraved forever in ink and in heart.

To my **readers**, who stayed with me through every twist, every tear, every pause thank you. Your patience, your messages, your warmth gave me the courage to keep going. I'm sorry for the silence that crept in toward the end, but sometimes, even writers fall apart. Your support means more than I can ever express.

To those who believe in second chances and silent prayers, this book is for you.

To the friends who heard me out at 3 a.m., the ones who read my drafts, the ones who believed in Ataraxia and Cherish as much as I did thank you for holding me when I couldn't hold myself.

And lastly, to **the unknown tomorrow**, where healing happens, where stories return, and where part two will rise... I am coming back. Stronger. Softer. Wiser.

Until then, keep your heart open, your faith alive, and your hopes intact.

Because the most beautiful stories are the ones that aren't finished yet.

With all my love,
**<u>Pranay Sawarkar</u>**